The Key to a Dynamic Church Life

Rune Brännström

Except where noted, all Scripture quotations are taken from the King James Version, public domain in the United States of America. All others are marked as indicated below:

God's Word Translation - GW
American Standard Version - ASV
International Standard Version - ISV
Good News Bible - GNB
Contemporary English Version - CEV
1912 Weymouth New Testament - WNT
1965 Bible in Basic English - BBE
English Standard version - ESV
Literal translation of the Holy Bible - LITV
New International Version – NIV
Jubilee Bible - JUB
1898 Young's Literal Translation - YLT

Cover Artwork: Kristian Lynn Villareal

Printed by CreateSpace

ISBN-13:978-1533642332
ISBN-10: 1533642338

Nehemiah Initiative Publisher

12531 Course View
San Antonio, Texas 78221, USA

ORDER ON LINE:

Amazon.com, CreateSpace.com
and other retail outlets

Search: Rune Brannstrom
or the title

To order in bulk; contact the publisher

DEDICATION

I dedicate this book to my children:

To Susanna, who is planting a church in London, England and residing there with a team that she leads.

To Daniel, who is the father of four children and working withhis new company. He is also doing volunteer work in the Swedish Christian school that he started nine years ago.

To Christina, who is the mother of four children and director of five Swedish Christian thrift shops that support mission for children.

To Magdalena, who is working in early childhood education in Oslo, Norway and active in her church.

To Johanna, who is a mother of three children and works as a high school counselor. She is also engaged in politics in Sweden and is active in her church.

ENDORSMENTS

“Rune's book is a gift sent from the Lord. After just the first hundred pages my spirit burned with joy for the testimonies recorded, the inspirational vision and the hope for the future.

I think it is an incredibly timely book which focuses deeply on the most important aspects of Christianity, such as love and the Holy Spirit, in a way that brings us into and prepares us for the new critical time in which Jesus has placed us.
Get ready!!!!!”

Allan Parker
Justice Missionary
President, The Justice Foundation

“When Francis Galton invented the dog whistle back in 1876, it was a breakthrough. This new device emitted an ultrasonic sound that animals could hear - including dogs and cats - but no humans. In much the same way, Rune Brannstrom is prophetically releasing a proclamation...a message...a pronouncement...a heavenly sound that is offered to those that *"have an ear to hear!"*

His words confirm and have brought a definite clarity and confirmation to what has been stirring in my heart. The church is on the precipice of a "Love Revolution," of unprecedented proportions that will be contained in a new wine skin of church life that the church has not experienced since it's birthing.

I encourage you to take this book into your prayer closet and prayerfully read the words, meditating on God's love for you - and His love for those surrounding you. This book exhorts us to realize, recognize and release the greatest commandmentfound in Matthew 22:37-38, *"You shall love the Lord your God with all your heart, and with all your soul, and with all your mind. This is the great and foremost commandment. The second is like it, You shall love your neighbor as yourself."*

Billy Nunez
Associate Pastor - Keys Vineyard Community Church,
Florida Keys, FL, USA

"Pastor Rune is a Dynamic leader and teacher. His teachings have brought tremendous insight to many including myself. He challenges Christians to rethink how they are doing church and begin to think kingdom.

Keys to the Dynamic Church Life will give you deep insight to how God intended us to live out our Christian walk together as a body of believers.

Be prepared for a paradigm shift as you read this book. Once you start, you won't be able to put it down. I pray that God will speak to your spirit as you read each page and that your life will be forever impacted as mine was".

Mark Lugo
Founder and Director, iFamily

“Keys to the Dynamic Church Life is refreshing and revelational. Rune's wisdom and insight opens the reader's understanding of what being a part of the Body of Christ is all about. No more church as usual, Jesus is ushering us into the new paradigm of what church-life is all about. This is a must read for all pastors who are tired of the old pattern of "doing"church”.

Bryan L. Thomas
Pastor and Founder of SWEEP over San Antonio

“Pastor Rune shares in his new book, “God’s home is not a structure – a physical house. No, His home is His people who enjoy Him and one another in loving family relationships.” Perhaps, this statement dynamically exemplifies the very heart of Pastor Rune---and the heart of this new book.

This minister of the Gospel who has his thumb on the ‘pulse’ of the church shares deep understanding of the make-up of today’s church.

More than a building, a structure, or a group of people, it is the Lord Himself infusing His glory and character into a God-hungry society. Pastor Rune relates this evolution with great wisdom and insight. Prepare to be greatly blessed by this powerful account of the unfolding glory of God’s church”.

Ruben Duarte
President, Into His Presence Ministries

“There is a lot of talk today about how to get our modern churches to awaken unto the life and power that was normal for the book of Acts church. Many are not satisfied with things as they are and acknowledge that change must ensue. In searching for answers as to why there is such a drastic difference between the early church and now, the majority of the conversation (that I have seen) has been largely focused on the *form* and not the *substance.*

In his book; Keys To The Dynamic Church Life, Apostle Rune Brannstrom powerfully and clearly brings the *substance* of the New Testament Church to the forefront of the conversation. Apostle Rune clearly lays out the heavenly blue-print for what normal church life looks like: A *daily* lifestyle of love for Jesus and His body, the church. Rune writes with a father's heart calling sons and daughters into ground he has taken in the Spirit. He does not present any theory, but he testifies of what he walks in and has lead others into. We would be wise to so alsofollow."

David Lee Brown
Director, SA Tabernacle House of Prayer

CONTENTS

SECTION ONE
A New Paradigm

SECTION TWO
The Nature of the Church

SECTION THREE
The Four Keys to New Testament Church Life

SECTION FOUR
Deeper Revelation

Preface

A while back my wife Berta and I had lunch after a Sunday service with some good friends who were visiting from Florida. They had just been guest ministers at our local church.

They are amazing worship leaders as well as ministers of the Word and of prophecy. Yet although we greatly value their gifts, these are not the main reason we cherish these two people. Although we see each other perhaps only once or twice a year these days, we have about 15 years of history together during which time our lives have been irreversibly intertwined during times of joy and laughter as well as times of great pain in the inevitable trials and tests of life.

In short, we have seen the good, the bad and the ugly. Yet, never was there a doubt about our love and commitment to one another. When we reunite, no matter how much time has passed, we take up right where we left off.

We realize that there is something about true friendship in the Body of Christ, that speaks so loudly and clearly of the love of Jesus. That genuine love that provides the safe place to be real and vulnerable; the place to fail but then to be healed and restored; the place to be affirmed in your true worth and lifted into godly boldness; the place where perfect love truly casts out all fear.

Although it may sound cliché, the world is starving for one thing: **the love of God**! Even much of the Body of Christ is still walking around wounded and in bondage because they have not encountered the true heart of Jesus in their churches.

So much pain, brokenness, and needless casualties have occurred because of the lack of freedom and security in the Church that only the genuine love of God can provide.

The spirit of religion has kept pastors and members of many churches in bondage. Instead of the healing grace of God, legalism has produced the fear of rejection, the fear of failure and the pressure to perform. So many of God's children have come out of the tomb but are still walking in their grave clothes. Who will love them enough to loosen them?

But, hallelujah, God is doing a new thing today in the Ecclesia, which is God's elect, the Body of His Dear Son, Jesus Christ!

There is a supernatural joy and a peace that is getting ready to overtake God's people as a baptism of the love of God is poured out upon them. The goodness of God is becoming so tangible and visible among those that love one another with the love of Jesus that it cannot be contained! It will surely overflow onto a thirsty humanity who will at last be able to taste and see that the Lord is GOOD!

SECTION ONE

A New Church Paradigm

God's plan of redemption through Christ is not just restoring our lost fellowship with God, but also restoring our capacity to truly love our fellow believers

Chapter One

The Problem

The New Testament promises[1] a life filled with power and authority. We are assured that we are more than conquerors in all things and that we have been given the abundant life and the living water which will cause us to never thirst again.

However, how many Christians sitting in our churches today are truly satisfied with their lives? How many, instead, feel that they are missing something; something that they had expected when they gave their lives to the Lord?

They seem to always be seeking after that one thing that will finally bring them the fulfillment their hearts long for. This quest can lead to dissatisfaction and "church hopping" with no fulfilling results.

[1] Acts 1:8, Luke 10:19, Romans 8:37, Ephesus 3:19, John 6:35, John 10:10

This does not negate the genuine new birth with the open channel to a personal relationship with God. Nevertheless, for many the deep basic needs that were left unmet in their lives prior to conversion still remain unmet in many ways.

A person who has become a believer can be tempted to ask themselves, "Am I living the abundant life? If so, why am I still hungry and thirsty?"

We need other Christians

The fact is that the Christian life was never meant to be lived "solo" or in isolation. The person who says, "Well, it's just me and Jesus, and that's all I need" is living a myth.

Christ's family is His Body, and we cannot have a deep satisfying relationship with the Head that meets the deepest needs of our souls, without genuine, meaningful relationships with His Body, His people.

It is sharing life with Him who is the Head and with the Church which is His Body that gives the fullness of joy that the Lord wants all people to experience.

God wants our hearts to be satisfied

Paul shows us the way to a fulfilled life in Colossians 2:2. He says . . . *"that their hearts may be encouraged, being knit together in love, to reach all the riches of full assurance of understanding and the knowledge of God's mystery, which is in Christ,"*. (ESV)

The fulfilled life, where I have all I need can only be experienced as I, together with other believers, melt to be one heart and one mind. The corporate life we enjoy together in Jesus Christ is what brings us into a deep understanding and knowledge of God. No amount of personal study can substitute for the revelations God will give those who are willing to yield their hearts toward genuine koinonia in the Holy Spirit.

The Lord longs for us to experience joy and fulfillment. That was His original intent for the biological family. That is also His purpose for the Church today.

That is also Paul's message in Ephesians 3:18-19; *"This way, with all of God's people you will be able to understand how wide, long, high, and deep his love is. You will know Christ's love…so that you may be completely filled with God."*. [2]

The Power of Koinonia

Church services can be a powerful blessing, and as I read the Bible in my devotions, I can hear God speak to me. Furthermore, I can see God act in response to my prayers. Yet the fact remains that a full and satisfied life

[2] GW

can only be attained through walking out my destiny in God with brothers and sisters that I love and that I know love me. This kind of koinonia (fellowship) cannot be contrived; it must be birthed by the Holy Spirit.

My wife and I have experienced these kinds of relationships most of our Christian lives, even before we met and were married. In recent years we have come into a rich fellowship with a team of people who are working together in a ministry called the Nehemiah Initiative, a prayer/evangelism non-profit.

The original team consists of brothers and sisters who bonded together in 2009-2010 by praying daily on site for a year for a specific crime ridden and spiritually dark area of our city. We then launched an evangelistic campaign in this area during which we saw the Lord make a significant impact which is still being felt today.

This shared experience was not without the challenges of intense resistance from the Enemy, but even the suffering served to bond us together.

Through this experience the Lord produced a love in us for one another that has been a fertile ground for others to come in and be planted into.

These newcomers often remark about how good it is to be able to feel the freedom to be real and transparent with one another and know that we have one another's backs.

This same Nehemiah Initiative team is also part of a larger group of pastors and intercessors who have been worshipping together with us every Tuesday morning for sixteen years.

At these Tuesday meetings worship is always gloriously powerful. We also give room for the prophetic, for intercession, for the sharing of the Word or for ministering to one another. The beautiful thing is that, although we are all leaders, there is no competition or jealousy among us. We see one another after the Spirit and celebrate one another's gifts and welcome them being activated.

Because of the strong bond and commitment to one another other, we have been able to welcome visiting missionaries and ministers into a rich atmosphere of God's love and "wash their feet". We work in harmony as a ministry team to bring encouragement, comfort and edification to men and women of God.

Also, several pastors and ministers who have come to visit have been hooked and continued to be part of the group for years because of the deep need that it meets in their lives. Two of the more recent additions, apastor and an evangelist, have remarked, "You don't know how long I have been longing for such a group where I could connect with other leaders and feel safe and athome!"

The simple but powerful fact is that **God has knit us together in love!** Our unity and our sincere love for one another have built a home where God is pleased to dwell.

This is what God wants for any local Church or ministry. Paul tells us this very clearly; *"you also are built together for a dwelling place of God".*

God wants us to build Him a home in our city![3]

Our religious minds find it difficult to believe that Almighty God would want to "hang out" with His children simply because He delights in us! But the truth is that God has always longed to dwell among His people and to find a place where He feels at home on this earth.[4]

God's home is not a structure – a physical house. No, His home is His people who enjoy Him and one another other in loving family relationships.

If God had a home in your City what would it look like?

Let me share with you my heart's picture of God's home in a city.

When you walk near God's Home, you hear wonderful music that draws you and makes you wonder: "what is going on in there?" You hear sounds of joy and laughter. As you go in the front door, there is a giant family room. It is filled with sons and daughters of God of all ages and from different denominations, traditions and ethnicities.

---

[3] Exodus 25:8, Ephesus 2:21-22
[4] Exodus 25:8

Their faces are glowing and you understand that this comes from the glory of the Father.

In the center of the family room you see the Father smiling with a look of such joy and satisfaction. He is surrounded very closely by sons and daughters who have been away for years but now have come back to their Father.

They can't seem to get enough of His nearness. As they wipe away tears of joy and gratitude from their eyes, they know they are home to stay!

Lots of other sons and daughters are also in the family room enjoying fellowship with the Father and with one another. They rejoice to see the newcomers' ecstatic faces as they gaze upon Papa's face, and they are so glad to have played a part in bringing them home to Him.

The father has thrown a great party for them and He knows how to party! Love, Joy and Peace are being poured out and served by the glass. Fruit and flowers are everywhere and from the kitchen a scrumptious aroma stems from what is baking in the oven and cooking on the stove. This fills us with anticipation of the good things to come!

In the kitchen and all around the house people are sharing exciting testimonies of miracles, signs and wonders. Some are sharing new songs, or art work, or writings, or witty inventions, or business ideas the Spirit has given them. The atmosphere is buzzing with creativity!

Others are sharing of the faithfulness of the Father carrying them, sustaining them and bringing them through seemingly impossible deserts. As they share, many wounded and battle weary saints are refreshed and encouraged.

Although there are many present, every individual person is aware of the tangible personal love of the Father and throughout the house they see things that have personal significance and meaning to their hearts because the Father has placed them there to show how perfectly He knows and loves each of His children.

They are all aware that there are many more sons and daughters that have not yet come home. They also know that the Holy Spirit will empower and guide them to reach out to them.

But more than anything, they know that it is the love they are partaking of here in Papa's House that is the most powerful weapon for disarming the Enemy and setting the captives free!

Emma

The story of Emma is a wonderful example of how the love of the Father manifested through His family can penetrate all barriers.

Back in the early 90's my wife, Berta, and I were pastoring a church in Sweden. Swedes tend to be very private and reserved individuals and for the most part very secular.

Our son Daniel together with a team of young people began an afterschool program in order to reach out to the children in the neighborhood because it was an easier way to eventually reach their parents.

One little girl named Emma became a regular in the after school activities at the church. Emma was about ten years old and she and her younger brother were being raised by a single mother, Birgitta, who was a nurse.

That spring we planned our annual church family retreat that was attended by most of the congregation. The schedule was usually filled with fun activities that parents, children, youth and singles could participate in together, including a variety talent show at the end of the week-end. In addition, there was a lot of good food and wonderful fellowship at meal times. Of course, there were also Bible studies and rich times of worship in the Lord's presence.

On that particular retreat, we brought along some of the neighborhood children with their parents' permission. Emma was among them and she was powerfully touched over the week-end by the rich loving atmosphere among the family of God.

She received the Lord and returned home to her mother a totally transformed child. She asked to be among those being baptized the following week and her mother came to her baptism and took pictures.

Not long after this, we started what is called an Alpha course for the purpose of reaching non-Christians with the gospel. This is a series of classes and each session begins with a dinner, then a presentation of an aspect of the Gospel and lastly, dessert and small discussion groups.

We got a call at the church office from Birgitta saying, "I'm calling to register for this Alpha course. I haven't the slightest idea what it is, but my daughter Emma has begged me to take it, saying she doesn't want a birthday or Christmas gift; all she wants is for me to join this class. So I guess I'm in".

Birgitta fulfilled her promise to Emma and was gloriously saved the second week!

Because Swedes tend to live isolated and private lives, there is often a loneliness that permeates their lives that they just accept as normal. However, this course, with the sharing of a hot meal which was ready for them as they came directly from work, and the atmosphere of fellowship in the presence of God, stirred a need deep within the hearts of these unchurched Swedes that disarmed their usual guardedness.

When the course was almost finished and Berta announced that next week would be the last session, their faces revealed a deep disappointment. One man said, "you can't do that to us!" After several weeks everyone wanted to continue!

Out of the 25 people who attended the Alpha course, 21 were baptized in water including Birgitta! This time a jubilant ten-year old Emma took the pictures of her mom making a public profession of her faith in Jesus Christ!

A follow-up discipleship class was planned which they all attended! Although we didn't serve a dinner, we had refreshments and folks continued to cultivate the new relationships they had made.

The beautiful by-product of this experience was that the team of church members that worked together to host this course also bonded in an even deeper relationship with one another. God had used them together to help bring these lost souls into the Father's family.

We then started a new Alpha course and got the same results! This was so unusual for Sweden that we were written about in an article which appeared in a national Christian magazine!

Birgitta became a committed member of our church and a wonderful addition to the church family. She went on to get training as a Christian counselor and was a tremendous blessing to many!

What was the key to this amazing series of events? It was a loving church family where Jesus stirred the need in lonely people for His love and then fulfilled it through His Body!

Without close relationships, we will not experience a fulfilled life.

As humans created in God's image we are made for relationships, first with Him and then with one another. There is nothing that can take the place of healthy, solid, genuine relationships with brothers, sisters, spiritual mothers and spiritual fathers. Without this the Christian life can feel empty and meaningless.

From the beginning, the Lord has longed for us to experience joy and fulfillment. That was also His original intent for the biological family and is also His purpose for the Church today. It was and is His desire that the Church would be an extended family of rich relationships characterized by love, loyalty, care for one another's needs, and joyful sharing of life.

When sin came into the world, this not only caused the breaking of man's relationship with God but also fractured mankind's ability to have the healthy relationships that God intended.

Cain killed his brother Abel because of jealousy and then was doomed to a life of loneliness separation from the family of his birth and from God.

If one were to ponder what one of the torments of hell might be, I believe among these would be isolation and desperate loneliness without the hope of relief. Unfortunately, this is the plight of many people still on this earth!

God's plan of redemption through Christ, however, does not just restore our lost fellowship with God our Father, but through the healing of the soul, also gives people the capacity to love one another as our Creator intended. This is a taste of heaven on earth and the fabric of the New Testament Church family.

Both the Evangelicals and the Charismatics, as well as the mainline churches are at a point of a needed radical transformation

Chapter Two

A Second Reformation is Emerging Today

A few of months ago as my wife, Berta, and I entered our church sanctuary on a Sunday morning, a certain new couple who had seated themselves on the back row caught our eye.

Berta, being the enthusiastic greeter of new people that she is, immediately went over to them.

To her surprise, she recognized them as a couple we had met 16 years ago when we had just moved to San Antonio from Sweden but we had not seen them since. Their names were Eli and Tina.

They had been members of another church at the time we first met and had been very active and very devoted. As it turns out, they had a couple of heartbreaking and devastating experiences with "church" and had just stopped going for years. They had not stopped loving the Lord; they had just checked out of "church" as they had known it.

In fact, they had already sold their house and made plans to move to another town in south Texas with the hope of maybe finding what they needed and longed for among relatives there.

However, the week before they were scheduled to move, Tina's sister, Alice, and her husband, Gus, had visited our church. They too had felt rootless and disconnected from church for years.

In many ways, our church is not very different from other non-denominational charismatic churches. But one thing my wife, Berta, and I have prayed for during many years, is that we would raise up a people who would truly become a family because this is what we ourselves had experienced in the past and this is what we saw in the New Testament scriptures. We knew in our hearts that it was what the Lord also longed for.

Thanks be to God, after some years, we have begun to experience this level of love and commitment among our core members like never before.

We see the Lord healing and affirming His sons and daughters through spiritual mothers and fathers and encouraging them through brothers and sisters. It has led to a surge of new people coming and wanting to connect because their hunger for the authentic Church is being stirred.

Alice and Gus were among these and as it turns out, they experienced something refreshing and uplifting in our church. They met genuine, friendly people and a sense that they had come home.

They encouraged Tina and Eli to join them the following Sunday. That was the day of our re-encounter with Tina and Eli who also heard the Lord in a fresh new way during the service and sensed that God was holding them back from moving to another town.

Since then, both couples have become members of our church and are part of a home fellowship hosted by Eli and Tina. The joy and the renewed hope in the hearts of these precious people is so moving to see.

Their hunger for the Word and for the presence of God is strong and deep. They are building new relationships and also quickly becoming wonderful mentors for some of the new believers who have joined their homegroup.

They, as well as many others, are tapping into the living Body of Christ and discovering the fountain of life that is flowing from the Father to his children when they love one another.

A Second Reformation is Emerging Today

This book is about the true nature and the organic expression of the Church that was birthed on the Day of Pentecost 2000 years ago and the need to return to it. The focus is not on external changes that the Church needs to make.

However, a new understanding of the true nature of the New Testament Church will bring revelation that will transform our expression of it.

The paradigm that the typical local church has developed in the Western world over the past century has reached a crisis point.

The model of a senior pastor having the platform every Sunday morning trying to keep the sheep fed and content so that they keep coming and keep giving, is no longer working. The pressure to grow the church by making the "worship" more appealing and providing better children and youth programs, making smarter use of technology and more seeker friendly services usually only serves to draw sheep from other houses or to entertain seekers without bringing them into a true understanding of the gospel.

In fact, even the sheep that have been in church for decades are often not scripturally literate and have no revelation of the gospel of the kingdom of God that Jesus spent His time on earth preaching.

Neither the pastor nor the sheep can sustain this routine indefinitely without a sense of emptiness, dissatisfaction and burnout.

Consequently, we have seen a mass exodus of people leaving the local churches, especially youth and young adults. Both mainline and non-denominational churches have been losing members at an alarming rate.

According to researcher George Barna 20 million adults throughout the nation have left the established Church[5] (1999). Furthermore, scores of pastors throw in the towel every year.

George Barna explains[6]: "A common misconception... is that they are disengaging from God when they leave a local church. We found that while some people leave the local church and fall away from God altogether, there is a much larger segment of Americans who are **currently leaving churches precisely because they want more of God in their lives but cannot get what they need from a local church.**[7] They have decided to get serious about their faith by piecing together a more robust faith experience. Instead of going to church, they have chosen to be the Church in a way that harkens back to the Church detailed in the Book of Acts".

The above report is startling; **people have to leave the local church to find more of God and to get serious about their faith!**

---

[5] https://www.barna.org/component/content/article/5-barna-update/45-barna-update-sp-657/170-a-faith-revolution-is-redefining-qchurchq-according-to-new-study#.V22iBNc0Dv8

[6] https://www.barna.org/component/content/article/5-barna-update/45-barna-update-sp-657/170-a-faith-revolution-is-redefining-qchurchq-according-to-new-study#.V22iBNc0Dv8

[7] The emphasis by author

Does this mean that God has left the traditional Church with its outreach to the community?

No! But the traditional Church is at a crossroad. It must decide if it wishes to defend its traditions or move on with God.

Both the Evangelicals and the Charismatics as well as the mainline churches are at a point of a needed radical transformation.

We are living in the midst of epic changes in our society sparked in recent years by technological developments as well as the disintegrating moral fiber of our nation. This has also greatly affected the Church.

Furthermore, the Church has also entered a new phase since the third millennium began. We are leaving the Church age behind us and are entering the Kingdom age.

What does this Kingdom paradigm entail?

Simply put, people are no longer satisfied to be pew warmers. Christians all over the nation are understanding that God has given every born-again child of God delegated authority to be a minister of reconciliation. The mission is to advance the gospel and the culture of the Kingdom of Heaven wherever we go. The goal is that the lost may be drawn to the King Himself, and that His reign and rule might be established on earth.

Our heart's cry is *"Thy kingdom come; Thy will be done on earth as it is in heaven![8]"*

To live on the cutting edge of the new things that God is doing today, we need to understand the true nature of the Church and by the Spirit of God give birth to the New Testament Church life.

The Second Reformation

A second reformation is emerging in our day. It is all about giving birth to the authentic Biblical Church life in traditional local churches as well as in house churches.

The first reformation of the Church in the 1500's gave birth to the Protestant movement. Martin Luther ignited it by his 95 theses (1517).

That reformation was about creeds; salvation by grace through faith apart from works. The second reformation is not about what the Church believes, but about her life and nature.

Any local Church that wants to be a part of that reformation will have a problem identifying it through its structures and programs. Only by its nature can it be perceived.

The hidden secret

[8] Mathew 6:10

The present-day reformation is a hidden secret in the pages of the New Testament. To find it, we must become seekers like Abraham who; *"looked for a city which hath foundations, whose builder and maker is God"*[9].

The Church was and is that City that Abraham was seeking after![10]

Present day Church leaders must become seekers after the true Church nature and life in order to rediscover the life that is revealed in the New Testament.

Jesus said; *"Seek and you will find"*[11].

This book is all about rebirthing the true Church.

It is a fallacy to believe that the Body of Christ can be inherited from one generation to the next.

The Church is not an organization. Jesus Christ's Body on this earth is a living organic spiritual body that needs to be birthed into every new generation by genuine conversions and fresh revelations of God Himself and of His purpose for His people on this earth.

The secret of God's Church

[9] Hebrew 11:10 KJV
[10] Matthew 5:14, Revelation 21:9-10
[11] Matthew 7:7 CEV

This book will give you some insight into God's secrets about the Church that are revealed in the New Testament.

The Bible tells us; *"yea, if you cry after knowledge and lift up your voice for understanding; if you seek her as silver, and search for her as for hidden treasures, then you shall understand...and find the knowledge of God."* [12]

Jesus said, "Only you can know the secret truth about God's kingdom". [13]

---

[12] Pro 2:3-5 MKJV
[13] Mar 4:11 ERV

The light of the Holy Spirit is the key for the modern Church to come into an experience of the Normal New Testament Church life.

Chapter Three

Welcome to the New Testament Church paradigm

The Christians in the first century experienced unprecedented success. The power and the life in that church has become a model throughout church history. Many churches today have lost that dynamic quality of church life. For that reason, they have also lost tens of thousands of their people who find church to be irrelevant to their lives.

Nevertheless, there is definitely still a powerful hunger and thirst in human beings for what God intended the Church to be.

However, the typical lost person would never think to look to the Church to fill that deep ache in his heart.

Why? Because that dynamic quality of authentic Church life which satisfies the deep needs of the human soul seems to be lacking in so many local churches.

Even the mega churches which on the surface seem extremely successful are not meeting people at the point of their deepest need.

Yet the Lord has given us some glimpses over the last few decades of the Church life that brings heaven to earth.

The Charismatic renewal

In the 60's and 70's an interesting phenomenon occurred in Body of Christ as a by-product of the outpouring of the Spirit known as the Charismatic renewal in which millions of people in the Catholic Church and other mainline denominations all over the world experienced what the Bible calls the baptism in the Holy Spirit[14].

The Spirit produced a fervent love for God and released through His people a powerful love for one another. One could almost say that it closely resembled what life must have been like in the new born Church after the first Pentecost.

This led to the emergence of Christian communities in which spirit-filled Christians lived in various living situations and shared daily life together.

[14] Acts 1:4-5,8, 2:1-4

Some of these living situations consisted of a married couple with or without children together with some single people. Other homes consisted of only single men or of only single women. But mainly the communities were made up of nuclear families who shared life with other nuclear families whose children experienced the richness of an extended family of children and adults.

In every case, the goal was to share daily life in the richness of corporate worship, prayer, scripture study, fellowship and mutual support and encouragement in growing in the knowledge of God and of their identity in Him.

Even though they did not necessarily engage in what is considered classic evangelistic outreach, they nevertheless added to their number on a consistent basis simply by relational evangelism. This entailed, for example, having conversations with co-workers or students on campus and inviting them to dinner in homes and Bible studies or worship gatherings.

One such community was started by college students in the late 60's in the university town of Ann Arbor, Michigan. My wife Berta who moved to Ann Arbor in 1973 to attend graduate school at the University of Michigan was radically converted and transformed through this community. There was a dynamic move of God that touched hundreds of young adults and eventually had a powerful international impact which drew visitors from many Hispanic, Asian, and European nations.

Why? Because there was something about the depth of love and the quality of commitment to one another among these Christians that was so distinct from anything that one could experience in any other Christian setting.

When Berta first came there to attend the University of Michigan, she had only had some minimal experience of the concept of God as a child through the Catholic Church. In fact, as a young adult she had been experiencing a deep emptiness and sense of meaninglessness that had led her to explore New Age practices.

What she found among these born again, spirit filled young people in the community was the visible and tangible presence of God in the manner in which they loved, honored, served and just simply enjoyed life together in the Lord.

They were not stiff or religious; in fact, there was an amazing authenticity, freedom, a sense of humor, and joy that Berta had never experienced among her non-Christian friends even in their so-called "partying" life-style.

There was also the incredibly charged atmosphere that came when they corporately worshipped the Lord with music and song in their general assemblies. Much of the music was written by members of the community many of whom had been music majors at the university.

Berta is convinced that words alone would not have been enough to pierce her heart. What deeply touched her and made her ready for the gospel message was the taste of Heaven she experienced in God's presence both in the worship and in sharing meals and interacting in a natural way with people who loved God and who were committed toward loving one another with the heart of Jesus.

This community had over 2000 members by the late 80's. They also arranged and carried out international charismatic conferences attended by tens of thousands of spirit-filled people.

Berta attended one such conference in 1974 at Notre Dame University where 30,000 people filled the football stadium. This is where her actual conversion took place as she saw healings and miracles and a people passionately in love with Jesus and with one another even though they came from different cultures and nations.

What was God doing through this group of young people? I believe He was giving a picture of the New Testament Church.

The Community in Malmö, Sweden

Ann Arbor was not the only such community. In the early 80's, I myself experienced this life in Sweden where a community of 150 people transformed the environment and spiritual atmosphere of a large apartment complex located in a part of town that was one of the least desirable.

As was stated before, Swedes tend to be very reserved and private people and not usually open to just any stranger. Furthermore, most have a very secular world view. But as in all humans, there is that inner ache in them for what only God can satisfy.

God has hidden mystery in the scriptures but He wants to give it to our hearts as a revelation.

That longing got stirred up by the love of God manifested through the rich committed relationships among the families that shared daily life together in our community. This led to the salvation of people who would have otherwise never set foot in a church. What was the reason? They experienced the Word made flesh through God's people.

A further interesting detail is that the Malmö local government began to mention this apartment complex in their ads to attract residents, listing it as a wonderful, peaceful and safe place for families to live.

That led many non-Christian publications in Sweden to write articles of this unusual Christian community.

The community also got national exposure among the churches and denominations in Sweden through our national Christian conferences and magazine.

Through history, God's Church has had many expressions.

I am not saying that we all need to live in communities as described above, but the Church is in desperate need of that quality of genuine, transparent, God-centered relationships where hearts are healed and lives are rescued and restored by relating to true spiritual fathers and mothers and brothers and sisters thereby finding their self-worth and identity in God the Father.

In our society of broken homes and dysfunctional families, the Church is meant by the Lord to be that place where people can experience being embraced by that rich, deep, healing goodness of God Himself.

Where can we find the Normal Church Life?

We are once again in great need of finding the secrets of the New Testament Church.

The New Testament Church life is one of the deep mysteries of God. Paul tells us that in Ephesus 5:32; *"There is a deep secret truth revealed in this scripture, which I understand as applying to Christ and the church"*. (GNB)[15]

Many Christians do not understand that the normal New Testament Church life cannot be obtained by natural means. God has hidden this mystery in the scriptures but He desires to give us the revelation that will help us begin to release it through our spirits to one another.

[15] See also Ephesus 3:1-6 and Mark 4:11

The New Testament Church Life Starts in the Heart

The revelation of the Biblical Church starts in the heart. Paul tells us, that you and I have spiritual eyes in our hearts. With them we can see into the spiritual dimension where God has hidden his secrets.

When our hearts are enlightened by the spotlight of God, then we can understand the truth, not only with our minds, but we can also see that reality - the truth, with the eyes of our hearts.

Paul said; *"With the eyes of your hearts enlightened, you will know".* [16]

The light and the truth

For us to experience the reality of New Testament Church life, we must pray as King David prayed in Psalm 43:3; *"Send your light and your truth. Let them guide me. Let them bring me to your holy mountain and to your dwelling place".* (GW)

David did not just pray that God would send the truth. He prayed also that light would come to his heart and that the light would lead him to God's dwelling place.

God's dwelling place in the New Testament is the Church[17], and that holy mountain is the place of

[16] Ephesians 1:18 ISV

[17] Ephesus 2:21-22

governmental authority which is delegated by God to the ecclesia, His Church.

We cannot fulfill God's purpose on earth as His people without allowing His Spirit, through revelation, to form us into a powerful, dynamic Body filled with His life, the very Presence of God abiding in the midst of a people who sincerely love one another from the heart.

This is what the Apostle Peter is commanding us: *"Love each other with a warm love that comes from the heart. After all, you have purified yourselves by obeying the truth. As a result you have a sincere love for each other".*[18]

The most important key is the light of the Holy Spirit

The light of the Holy Spirit is the key for the modern Church to come into an experience of the normal New Testament Church life. We desperately need Him to illuminate our hearts and our understanding.

---

[18] 1Pe 1:22 GW

New revelation does not change the truth in the Bible, it changes our perception of it.

Chapter Four

Revelation Brings Paradigm Shifts

New revelation does not change the truth in the Bible, it changes our perception and understanding of it.

The modern church needs a paradigm shift concerning the Church and how to express the life that is in it.

In the history of humanity, we have had a lot of paradigm shifts that have changed our way of life.

The automobile, the train, and the airplane are some of the paradigm shifts that have changed our mobility and produced our modern way of life.

This woman will give you a new paradigm

How old is this woman?

By shifting perspective, she will be a young woman or an old woman.

A paradigm shift does not change the reality; it changes only our perspective. But the new perspective of the normal Church life in the New Testament will radically transform our way of expressing our life as a Church.

A hindrance for a new paradigm shift is our natural tendency to cling to the old paradigm that we have lived in for years.

The 21st century's believers see the Church as a building where Christians come together for different church services, meetings and programs.

Most churches today function like any other nonprofit organization in society.

One of the secrets of the first Church in Jerusalem is that the believers saw the Church as a totally new way of life.

It is true that many churches have a powerful ministry both to Christians and to the lost. But the life of the modern Church is institutionalized.

New Testament Christians did not just go to church, as a part of their lives. Church **was** their life. However, to experience the Church as a way of life, is foreign for most modern Christians.

It is very difficult for us to picture Peter on the day of Pentecost, after the Holy Spirit had come over the disciples with fire and three thousand new believers had been baptized, to then turn to the disciples and say; "This was a fantastic day, but I am going home now, see you next Sabbath at 11 o'clock"!

The Church – the New Way of Life

For the 1st century's believers, the Church was not just a place for teaching, prayer and serving God. Acts 2 tells us that the life that the three thousand new believers were baptized into, impacted their daily life and every aspect of it.

We see this in Act 2:44-46; *"all the believers were together and had all things common. And they sold possessions and goods and distributed them to all, according as anyone had need. And continuing steadfastly with one mind day by day in the temple, and breaking bread from house to house, they shared food in gladness and simplicity of heart".* (LITV)

The Church life

The Church life that was expressed among the first believers included fellowship in their homes, togetherness, commitment to each other, eating together and an extravagant love that made them willing to share their possessions.

Daily they met in the temple and in their homes, the two arms of the New Testament Church.

Our modern glasses
Color our view of reality

When we read about the Church in the New Testament, we do not realize that we read with glasses that are colored by cultures that are over two thousand years old.

Ancient Greece was the birthplace of our Western culture. The Roman Empire was powerfully influenced by the Greeks and spread their version of that culture to Europe and other places. For this reason, Classical

Greece is generally considered the cradle of Western civilization.

When we read about Church in the book of Acts, we as Westerners read with our Greek/Roman glasses without being aware of it.

For most people, the color of our Greek/Roman glasses makes us see "church" as an institution, like a hospital or school. Church becomes a building for meetings and programs where God's work gets done.

But the true meaning of "Church" is ecclesia, which is the Greek word for the Church. That word translated to modern English, signifies the people who have been called out from our society and set apart to become the people of God.

In other words, the Church is a people and Church life is the life we live and share together as that people of God.

God wants us to experience a paradigm shift that comes when we put off our modern glasses that are colored by the Greek/Roman cultures and put on the glasses of the old Biblical Hebrew culture.

Another Key is the Concept of Family

When we look at the word "Church" through the Hebrew glasses, we see Church as a **family**. We see unconditional love, covenant, loyalty, honor, unity, sharing one another's burdens and one another's joys. We see a multigenerational extended family in which everyone has a sense of belonging, security and identity.

The Biblical Hebrew culture

In the Old Testament God's spotlight is on the family. The focus for Noah, Abraham and all the other believers in the Old Testament was on what God was doing in their homes and families.

Abraham experienced God in his home and as a sheep farmer. Although he was not a "minister of the gospel", he is considered one of the greatest men of God in the Bible because of his faith response to the Lord and because he was called by God to be the **father** of countless descendants.

God's purpose was fulfilled through family. This came about when he and Sarah by faith miraculously gave birth to a son, Isaac, who through his son, Jacob, would produce twelve patriarchs and their families, the people of Israel.

Besides giving us the Savior, the Bible, and taking the light of the gospel to the Gentiles, this chosen people would have as its high calling to be the leader of the nations of the world at the end of the age. All this started with one **family!**

The book of Exodus

In the book of Exodus, the focus is also on the family. When the people of God was to come out from Egypt, every Jewish father was to slaughter a lamb and place the blood on the door posts. That was how the father redeemed his family. The redemption was of families not just individuals.

We find the same thing in the New Testament scriptures that also depict the Biblical Hebrew culture. The focus in the New Testament is not on what God did in the Temple or in the synagogue. The spotlight is on the homes. The word “house” (family) in the New Testament occurs 206 times.

The centrality of family is best depicted in the well-known parable of the prodigal son. It is all about a father and his two sons. The message in this story is not only about a repentant son coming home, it is about a father’s passion for reconciliation and restoration of relationship with his son. The central focus is family. In it Jesus revealed what is of the utmost importance in our Heavenly Father’s heart—relationship with his children and relationships among the sons and daughters in His family. This is why it is so grievous when the older brother’s reaction reveals his lack of love for his brother which was rooted in his lack of true relationship with his father.

Furthermore, when Jesus encountered Zacchaeus, He did not invite him to a meeting in the synagogue. He said to him; *“today I must stay at your house...And Jesus said to him, this day salvation has come to this house".* 19

In the Book of Acts, we also find that salvation and redemption is of families not just individuals.

That is what Paul tells the jailer in Philippi: *"Believe in the Lord Jesus, and you and your family will be saved." They spoke the Lord's word to the jailer and everyone in his home. At that hour of the night, the jailer washed Paul and Silas' wounds. The jailer and his entire family were baptized immediately".* [20]

For Paul salvation was not just an individual experience it was for the whole family. When we believe in the Lord, the promise is that our whole household will be saved. This is an amazing promise!

"His entire family was baptized"

An interesting fact in the expression *"his entire family was baptized"*[21] is that this man's family was not only his wife and children. The old classical family at this time was an extended family with grandparents, relatives, servants and other workers.

Everyone in this extended family came into salvation because the head of the family, the father, opens the way, through his God given authority. This has powerful spiritual implications about how God sees families and

[19] Luke 19:5, 9 MKJV
[20] Act 16:31-33 GW
[21] Act 16:33 GW

works through the father, when that man is aligned with God and His ways.

A father's blessing has monumental ramifications that can remain in motion for generations to come. Likewise, the words and actions of a neglectful or ungodly father can have devastating consequences on his descendants.

Is it any wonder that the enemy through media (sit-coms) does so much to undermine the place and dignity of the father of the family portraying him as a weak and incompetent buffoon?

The Culture of God

Just as the Lord has destinies for individuals, He also has destinies for families and mantels of authority and anointing that can be passed from generation to generation when ancestors are faithful to God.

Both the Old Testament and the New Testament cultures are characterized by their focus on extended families. We see that the Church, the Body of Christ, in each city in the Book of Acts and the epistles is one large extended family. This is a major indication of what God wants for His Church today.

SECTION TWO

The Nature of the Church

The New Testament Church was not an institution for meetings and church programs. Church was meant to be a family environment. The focus is love and relationship – period.

Chapter Five

What is Church life all about?

"You Gentiles are not foreigners or strangers any longer; you are now citizens together with God's people and members of the family of God". [22]

As was stated before, in God's eyes, Church is an extended family and He is the Father of that family.

The amazing thing is that God, our Heavenly Father, is our closest relative. He is closer than our wife or our husband, our children, or our mother and father.

[22] Ephesus 2:19 GNB

Furthermore, everyone in the Church is either our sister or our brother. In other words, the Church is our extended family.

The reality is that our spiritual relatives are more closely tied to us than our biological ones who do not know the Lord. For we share the Father's DNA, we are washed in the blood of Jesus and we are made one by the Spirit of God that has come to dwell in us.

> **New Testament Church is all about people, not a place you go to. Church is your extended family that you belong to!**

John 1:13 says; [we] *"were born not of blood, nor of the will of the flesh, nor of the will of man, but of God."*

In short, the New Testament Church is all about people, not a place where you go to participate in religious activities. Church is your extended family to whom you belong and that belongs to you!

Concepts like fellowship, relationship, unity, covenant and commitment are all important concepts and principles in the New Testament.

Those words are not used in the business world or in institutions like schools or hospitals. On the other hand, they are of utmost relevance to the family.

You do not start a family because you want a good business. The reason for family is not functional, but rather family is all about personal relationship.

God's intention was and is that every human being should live his/her whole life in a family where they could have the deep needs of their hearts met.

God has provided family life for everyone. Even if our natural families did not fulfill those deep needs, the Church family is where those needs are to be met.

The secret found in the New Testament Church life is that the early Christians were not just saved and blessed by God as individuals. They also began to live out their Christian lives corporately with spiritual brothers and sisters with whom they were deeply bonded.

Extended family vs. nuclear family

It is very difficult today to experience the normal New Testament Church life that has its foundation in relationship rather than in meetings and programs because it is against our modern culture.

In our modern culture, few people experience the benefits and the joys of an extended family. Because of the increased mobility that has emerged in past decades, as well as extreme busyness, we tend to live isolated and independent lives from other people and even from our relatives.

Many people have biological extended family members in the same town that they see only at funerals or weddings. To change our lifestyle is a big challenge for us.

Before the industrial revolution, a great number of Americans lived in rural communities. It was common place for the extended family to feel a bond and a responsibility for one another. Their homes were filled with relatives who shared life's duties as well as it's joys and hardships. Today, this is almost unheard of because it is not a part of our modern lifestyle.

In ancient times and cultures, the home was the center of people's lives. They worked in or close to their houses. They ate and relaxed together and had a very tight knit togetherness in their extended families.

Nothing could be further from the truth in our modern culture. We live in nuclear families: father, mother and children, and even in this small group there is often a lot of disconnection.

Many people today live in private homes with walled security fences. Few families eat together every day and the time of relaxation is focused on television, the internet, and video games.

Facebook, although it can be used in constructive ways, is most often a pseudo fellowship and a poor and shallow substitute for genuine relationships. Yet in many homes more hours are spent on Facebook than in authentic interpersonal relating.

We live in one place; work in another, and go to church in a third place. We also drive our children to all their activities in different locations. In reality, we have a hard and hectic life today compared to the people in the ancient cultures because we put forth so much effort for so little return in real soul fulfillment.

In summary, one can say that for the first Christians in the New Testament to experience a close relationship with other believers was not a difficult thing because it was already a part of their culture. Their natural family culture was already a culture of extended family. For God's people today, it poses a definite challenge, but God would not call us to do something if He did not have the provision of grace that we need to live it!

God intended to meet the deepest needs of our soul through the family that we are born into.

Chapter Six

Why is the New Testament Church Life So Important?

I think we all understand that as human beings we have deep needs in our natural soul life. If these needs are not met, we will experience painful psychological and emotional issues that affect our capacity to have a healthy self-image and to fulfill our purpose.

In the 1960's a terrible experiment was conducted in an orphanage.[23] Young orphan infants were fed and kept clean but deprived of any physical affection or attention

[23] Journal of Medical Association 278.11

from any other human being. The result was astounding! Within two months, half of them died! The rest died not long after being rescued. They could not live without love!

It is not enough for us to have our basic physical needs met. We also have needs in our souls and in our spirits. If those needs are not fulfilled, we will experience profound deficits and potentially catastrophic effects in our lives.[24]

Mass Murderers

The FBI has made a criminal profile of mass murderers. They found that a mass murderer is a sociopath that lives an isolated life and is incapable of having relationships with other people.

Somehow the deepest needs of his soul were never met by the family he was born into. More than likely his parents, grandparents and his ancestors for generations did not receive what they needed most from

---

[24] Today it is very difficult for a family to meet their children's need. Family life has changed dramatically because of the Industrial Revolution in the 18th to 19th centuries, Before the Industrial Revolution most people lived in small villages (in England 75%). They lived and often worked as a family, either in agriculture or as skilled craftsmen. Both mother and father and children were together 24/7. In 1800 only 3% of the world's population lived in urban areas, according to the Population Reference Bureau (PRB). Today, according to the United Nations Population Fund (UNFPA) the world is undergoing the largest wave of urban growth in history. In 2008, for the first time in history, more than half of the world's population lived in towns and cities. By 2030 this number will swell to almost 5 billion. But the fundamental shift in the social structure is not that the modern family has become urban. It is that the fathers and most mothers are working outside the home. The children are in day care, 4k education, grade school and in many cases after school programs as well. Many children spend more time in the institutions of our society than with their fathers and mothers.

their families. Relationship dysfunction tends to be passed on through the generations.

Only God can meet our unique spiritual need for redemption, but His intention was to meet the deep needs of our souls through our family relationships.

Mothers primarily nurture, and fathers give the much needed affirmation in identity: two extremely foundational needs for a healthy soul, be it male or female.

God's purpose for the Family

As was stated before, God's intention was to meet the deep needs of the human soul through our natural family.

Let me summarize the needs of our soul:

1. Unconditional Love - for who we are and not for what we do
2. Security
3. Belonging
4. Provision
5. Support
6. Sharing our life – our heart, joy and burdens
7. Affirmation
8. Identity
9. Training for life

A healthy family fulfills these needs and this has positive ramifications for the individual and for society as a whole, even if the family does not know the Lord.

Our society is suffering because of the breakup of the family.

- 80% of the U.S. prison population comes from foster care![25]
- Approximately 1 in 5 adults in the U.S. experiences mental illness in a given year.[26]
- 18.1% of adults in the U.S. experienced an anxiety disorder such as post-traumatic stress disorder, obsessive-compulsive disorder and specific phobias.[27]
- Among the 20.2 million adults in the U.S. who experienced a substance use disorder, 50.5%, 10.2 million adults - had a co-occurring mental illness.[28]

God's purpose for the extended Church family

In light of the catastrophic effects that the family breakdown and dysfunction has had on the souls of so many people in society, it is all the more crucial thatthe

[25] According to KIDSAVE
[26] NAMI, the National Alliance on Mental Illness
[27] NAMI
[28] NAMI

Church, the extended family of God step into its full manifestation of the love, acceptance, grace, nurturance and affirmation of the heart of Father God.

Laura

We have seen powerful examples in our congregation of people being healed, restored and raised up into their true identity as sons and daughters of God through experiencing the Church as family.

One such example is Laura. She grew up in a family of six sisters. Her father who gave her very little individual attention died when she was about ten. Her mother had great difficulty in nurturing her children in general, but she had an inordinate disdain for Laura for a reason no one knows. She rejected her from the time she was born and into adulthood. The sisters also were always at odds with one another and even cruel on many occasions.

Because of the painful home environment, Laura began to run away in her early teens. At age 15 she became pregnant. When she sought help at home, she was received with anger and severe rejection from her mother who swiftly threw her out.

Laura did not know Jesus at the time, and did not know where to turn, but the Lord looked after her. She was cared for through her pregnancy at a home for unwed mothers and then God provided a family who took her and her baby girl into their home after the child's birth.

About five years later, her little girl came in contact with a Christian woman who shared the gospel with her and led her to Jesus.

But life was not finished dealing its harsh blows Laura's way and when her daughter was only 16 years old she was abducted and brutally murdered. The pain, the grief and the horror that Laura endured without the comfort and consolation of her mother and sisters was beyond description and the trauma left a wound in her soul the size of a cavern.

When Laura came to our church many years later she was in her 50's. By nature, she is loving, friendly and good at making people laugh; but deep inside she still carried the grief that caused her to have anxiety attacks, suicidal thoughts, and even asthma.

As Laura began to come into the family environment of our church and to connect personally with spiritual mothers and sisters, something amazing began to happen. She began to develop a deep and genuine relationship with Jesus.

As her spiritual mothers and sisters loved her and nurtured her, the Lord began a beautiful work of deep healing and deliverance as she received in her soul the acceptance and unconditional love she had missed in childhood.

Laura was baptized in the Spirit and learned to enter into His presence in worship; she began to study and even memorize scripture.

Then after a few years the Lord did what no doctor or therapist could have done. Because of the strong love reservoir she now had, she could allow the Lord to go down deep where the most painful trauma was, the loss of her daughter.

He reminded her that her little girl had received Him and gave her the assurance that she was home safe and full of joy.

Laura made a monumental decision to take her daughter's ashes which she had kept in a mausoleum for over 20 years and plan a beautiful day of surrendering her into the Lord's hands and casting the ashes into the sea.

My wife, Berta who is one of Laura's spiritual mothers had the privilege of accompanying her on that day to the coast along with some other supportive people. Berta remembers Laura dancing on the beach in praise to God and says it was an amazing sight!

A healthy family is important for our society, even if they don't know the Lord

This is just one testimony of God's work of restoration in the lives of people that have connected with the wonderful healing work of God through a church family that loves one another in such a way that the broken and the lost can come in and find the open arms of Papa God. When the Church functions as God intended it to function, even the deepest of needs can be met! It is through finding the forgiveness, love, and acceptance of God among His people that the broken of this world find wholeness.

God meets our needs through His Church

What we see in the New Testament Church, is that every one's needs were met, both material and emotional as well as spiritual needs. The extended family relationship the first Christians had with one another and with our heavenly Father was the key.

The love of God that the first Christians had for each other became like a healing salve and every need was met by that love.

The testimony the first Church had was this: *"Nor was there anyone needy among them; for all who were owners of lands or houses were selling them, and were bringing the proceeds of the things which had been sold, and were placing them beside the feet of the apostles; and they were distributing to each, to the degree that anyone had need".* [29]

This was not Christian socialism or communism.
The communist says: "What is yours is mine". But the first Christians said: "What is mine is yours."

The first Church overflowed so much with the love of God that they chose to give generously to those who were in need among them. They were not operating in obedience to a command, but rather from a heart led by the Spirit of God.

[29] Act 4:34-35 EMTV

Ananias and Sapphira

On the other hand, we see the Apostle Peter's and God's dealings with Ananias and his wife Sapphira.

This was an example of two people who deviated from the Spirit and heart of Jesus in a time and environment where the love and glory of God was otherwise so generously manifested.

He and his wife sold some property and agreed to hold back some of the money they had pledged. They pretended to give it all because they wanted the glory.

We cry out for the glory but we don't understand the ramifications. The greater the presence of God's glory, the greater the importance of having a reverent fear of the Lord. Even though Jesus has opened the way to the Father by His shed blood, we cannot take the glory of God for granted especially if He is manifesting His Presence in an unusually powerful way as He was in the early Church.

Peter told Ananias; *"While you had the land, it was your own. After it was sold, you could have done as you pleased with the money. So how could you do a thing like this? You have not lied to men but to God".* [30]

Both husband and wife fell dead that day. Great fear came upon the Church and upon all who heard of this event.

---

[30] Act 5:4 GW

The consequences at that time for a heart that deviated from the heart of God among His people, and was lacking in the reverent fear of the Lord, were severe and swift.

However, for those whose hearts were one with Jesus and in one accord with one another, the power to save, heal and deliver was amazingly glorious! This is what the Lord desires to do in our day; may we surrender to living our lives for His glory without holding anything back!

The most important thing in Church is not church services, or even reaching out with the Gospel. It is to *"love one other"*

Chapter Seven

The Main Thing

If you ask people what the most important function of the church is, some will say it is to teach and disciple the church members. Some leaders will tell you that the most important thing for a church is to reach out with the Gospel to non-Christians. All of this is very important.

But Jesus gave us another answer; *"I give you a new commandment, that you love one another. As I have loved you, you should also love one another. By this all shall know that you are My disciples, if you have love toward one another.* [31]

Here Jesus speaks about a new Commandment and that commandment is specifically for the Church.

[31] John 13:34-35 MKJV

Crucial in the Old Testament are the ten commandments that were given to Moses for all human beings.

However, the most important thing for the Church is the 11th commandment; "*that you love one another. As I have loved you, you should also love one another.*" [32]

Jesus tells us, preaching is not how society will know that the Christians is followers of Jesus. The biblical advertisements that speaks higher then preaching is a Church that has members that is in deep love with each other.

This commandment to *"love one another"* is so important to God that you find those words 16 times in the New Testament!

Paul makes this point so starkly clear that it forces us to examine the priorities of our local church; for to ignore it is perilous!

"I may be able to speak the languages of human beings and even of angels, but if I have no love, my speech is no more than a noisy gong or a clanging bell. (2) I may have the gift of inspired preaching; I may have all knowledge and understand all secrets; I may have all the faith needed to move mountains---but if I have no love, I am nothing. (3) I may give away everything I have, and even give up my body to be burned ---but if I have no love, this does me no good". [33]

32 John13:34 MKJV

33 1Co 13:1 3 GNB

God's key for witnessing

The Lord gives us a key for witnessing that is revolutionary! He tells us that when the love of God is flowing among us: *"all shall know that you are My disciples".* [34]

How can everyone in a city know that true Christianity is there? What is the sign?

The common modern sign is church buildings and religious programs. However, according to Jesus, the Biblical sign of genuine Christianity is the love among God's people.

As was mentioned before, my wife, Berta, was a grad student at the University of Michigan in Ann Arbor 1973. She did not know the Lord but was an avid seeker of truth. She went along the path that many young people followed at that time who were spiritually hungry. She became involved New Age philosophies including transcendental meditation.

However, on a particular day, before her conversion, she was invited to a wedding of a young couple who were born again and spirit-filled Christians. They belonged to a Christian fellowship of university students and most of the guests were fellow Christians. The atmosphere of the presence of God in the praise and worship at the ceremony deeply touched her heart. She remembers feeling a warmth physically come over her from the top of her head to the soles of her feet. It was

[34] John 13:35 MKJV

a brand-new feeling that she did not understand, but it was amazingly lovely!

But even more impacting was the tangible presence of God's love in the way the friends related to one another.

She remembers big tears streaming down her face but not understanding what was happening to her. It was as if her heart was recognizing Someone she had long sought after, even though her mind did not fully understand Who that was. Yet she experienced Him in the kindness of the people around her. The love pierced through any intellectual stronghold that had previously resisted Christianity.

In the following days, she was invited to dinner by some of the young people in the fellowship. She remembers how the scales that had previously blinded her eyes began to fall off as she experienced a new sense of peace and goodness in the midst of men and women of God who loved one another with the love of Jesus.

This was more effective in preparing her heart to receive the gospel than any tract or preaching had previously been.

This is an excellent illustration that shows that the most important priority for a Church is not church services or even reaching out with the Gospel. These things are very important, but the priority in God's heart is for us to *"love one other".*

What is love?

Many Christians understand love the same way Hollywood portrays it in movies. For them love is an emotion that comes and goes.

"Hollywood love" is like an elevator, that goes up and down. Sometimes it's on the 10th floor and sometimes it's on the 3rd floor and sometimes it goes all the way down to the cellar!

According to Hollywood, that is the time to break up the relationship with your spouse. The marriage is dead when that wonderful love emotion is not there anymore.

But love is not just an emotion. Love is, first and last, a life that gives. The most well-known Bible verse teaches us that; *"God loved the world this way: He gave his only Son".* [35]

God did not love the world just emotionally. He did not tell His angels; "It's terrible that humans have opened themselves to Satan's captivity, oppression, and cruelty. I feel so sorry for them!"

God did not just love us with loving words or by sympathetic emotions. He loved us by giving us the best and most precious thing he had. He gave His Only Son for our redemption; He gave Himself holding nothing back.

---

[35] John 3:16 GW

Love yourselves

Jesus said; *"Love your neighbor as you love yourself".*[36]

Our self-love is the greatest love we have. But how do we love ourselves? Do we say to ourselves when we wake up in the morning and stand before the mirror; "You are the most fantastic person I know. I love you with my whole heart!". Maybe some people do this, but the most usual way of loving ourselves is by washing and clothing ourselves and by feeding our hungry stomachs. Self-love involves action.

Biblical Love

"We understand what love is when we realize that Christ gave his life for us. That means we must give our lives for other believers. Now, suppose a person has enough to live on and notices another believer in need. How can God's love be in that person if he doesn't bother to help the other believer"? [37]

Love releases the presence of God

"God is love". [38] That is His nature and because love is His nature, His expression of who He is will always be actions of love.

---

[36] Mat 19:19 GW

[37] 1John 3:16-17 GW

[38] 1 John 4:8

When a Church lives in love it releases His nature in such a way that people in and outside the Church see and feel the tangible manifestation of God.

This is the reality behind the words in Act 2:47; They *"were respected by all the people. More and more people were being saved every day, and the Lord was adding them to their group".*[39]

"And fear came upon every soul: and many wonders and signs were done by the apostles".[40]

When the Church obeys the 11th commandment, *"love one other"*, that obedience from the heart and for His sake, will activate God's presence.

This will change a city's spiritual atmosphere more powerfully and effectively than any program or outreach, and revival will be a reality.

Love releases transformation

One such transformation that we had the privilege of watching is Arleen. When we met her she was in her early 40's. She had lived the gay life-style all of her youth and her adult life.

When she first visited our church, it was to attend a course we were offering for those interested in exploring what Christianity was all about. She came to please a friend who had repeatedly invited her to church and also

---

[39] ERV
[40] Act 2:43 KJV

because she was in a lot of emotional pain. She had recently had a painful break-up of a relationship with a woman.

It was doubly painful because the woman had a baby boy, a toddler, who Arleen had helped care for since birth and whom she loved very much. Now she was also cut off from him.

In one of the sessions of the course, she heard the parable of the prodigal son and the Spirit of God came over her so powerfully that she wept deeply. She confessed that she always knew deep inside that the way she was living was wrong but didn't see a way out before. That night she experienced the love and mercy of the Father, surrendered her life to Jesus and started on the path to a miraculous transformation.

Arleen began to attend Sunday services and to experience the people of the congregation fully accepting her and welcoming her with open arms. She has said that she felt like she had come home.

There was a group of elderly ladies that took special care of her and took her in as a daughter. It didn't matter that she still dressed in less than feminine clothes. What mattered was that she had set her heart to know Jesus.

These ladies loved Arleen into the kingdom of God. They did not focus on outward appearance or her past life. They just loved her.

Today, Arleen is an outstanding woman of God. Her walk has not been without struggles, but then again, whose is? The remarkable thing is that she has come to understand the grace of God because she experienced it in a church family.

Arleen is respected by her biological family who has been amazed at her transformation. They had their doubts as to whether she would sustain her decision to follow the Lord. But she has continued to live a pure life devoted to Jesus; she is a worshipper, a giver and a servant of the Living God! A powerful testimony to all her relatives.

Furthermore, Arleen is greatly respected by all her co-workers who all know of her faith in Christ. In fact, several of them have sought counsel from her and she freely shares the gospel with them.

Over the years the woman with the toddler boy decided she wanted some freedom from caring for the child and began to allow Arleen to have him on the week-ends. It was a perfect opportunity for her to begin to bring the boy to church where he learned to praise the Lord and to participate in Sunday school.

The boy has continued to come to church with her and actually lives with her for long stretches of time. He is now a ten-year old son of God who knows and loves the Lord. Only God knows how Arleen's decision to follow Jesus has dramatically altered this child's path and rescued him from a life of deep darkness.

This transformation of Arleen did not become a reality through anointed preaching alone but by the love of God manifested through a church family that accepted her and loved her unconditionally and helped her to know her Father and who she is in Him. That is the Church in action.

Love Releases Miracles

I truly believe that the men, women and children in the Body of Christ today are called to a depth of love and unity that will release a level of faith for miracles even greater than anything we see in the Book of Acts. Through us the Lord will release healing, deliverance, raising the dead and multiplication of food.

Through His Church and its powerful restoring love, the Lord will raise up a brave and valiant people who will not yield to the spirit of fear in times of great darkness and distress; for God's Word assures us that perfect love casts out all fear. [41]

Instead, they will manifest Jesus Himself to a desperate world and with signs and wonders bring in a great harvest. Paul tells us it is *"faith working through love"* [42] that avails much.

The Lord is speaking clearly to His Church in these days about returning to what really matters. He is calling us back to His ultimate purpose for His people and that is

---

[41] 1 John 4:18

[42] Galatians 5:6

that we be conformed to His image and truly reflect who He is; and He is, above all else, **love.**

This sounds so basic and yet how many local churches see this as their main goal: to love God and to love one another. To do whatever it takes to live in peace and transparency with one another and to meet one another's needs.

The expression *"one another"* is one of the main areas of focus for New Testament Church teaching.

Chapter Eight

The Teaching Focus for the New Testament

Brian Hathaway did a research on the NT and he found that 44% of the contents of the New Testament letters are all about how we, as Christians, should relate to one another. If you compare this with how much is written about the spiritual gifts, you will be surprised. Only 4% in New Testament letters is about spiritual gifts.

Why is it that so much teaching in the New Testament deals with relationships?

The answer is: The New Testament Church was characterized by deep and close relationships.

Consequently, they needed a lot of teaching on how to relate so that life could be lived in a peaceful and harmonious way.

It is understandable that many people living in close proximity sharing their daily lives provides a perfect environment for potential conflict, disagreements and offense.
The "sandpaper" ministry begins and if we respond according to God's Word we make one another nice and smooth *"living stones".*[43] That explains why 44% of the teaching in the letters in New Testament is about relationships in the Church.

> **"One another" is the focus for New Testament Church teaching**

Nevertheless, the emphasis for the teaching in many Churches the last 20 to 30 years has not been on how to relate with brothers and sisters in the Church. Instead, most of the emphasis has been on how to relate to our spouses and to our children; that is, the nuclear family. This has been a good thing and very much needed, but it is also an indication of something else. That is the fact that most Christians do not invest deeply in relationships with brothers and sisters in the Church on a **covenant** basis. This is actually a foreign concept to a large portion of the Body of Christ.

They will relate on a social or functional basis. It is enjoyable to have a church picnic or potluck or to do an outreach to the community for back to school needs or

[43] 1 Peter 2:5

even street evangelism. But it is definitely another thing to have a sense of deep rooted commitment to one another for the long haul. This is why "church hopping" is so prevalent.

Also, it is not uncommon for people to see the pastor as disposable and replaceable; or for the pastor to be on the look-out for a climb up the ladder to a bigger church with better pay. Is this what God meant for His ecclesia?

In contrast, when we read the New Testament we find the expression *"one another"* is one of the main areas of focus of Church teaching. This expression *"one another"* occurs 59 times in the New Testament, and every time it is a command. This says a great deal about what is important to the heart of God and to thefulfilling of our purpose as His Church and His Bride!

We are commanded to:

"Live in harmony with one another"[44]
"Honour one another above yourselves"[45]
"Serve one another"[46]
"Bear one another's burdens"[47]
"Forgive one another"[48]
"Encourage one another"[49]
"Show hospitality to one another"[50]
"Pray for one another"[51]

---

[44] Romans 12:16
[45] Romans 12:10
[46] Galatians 5:13
[47] Galatians 6:2
[48] Ephesians 4:32
[49] Hebrews 3:13
[50] 1 Peter 4:9
[51] James 5:16

These are just a few examples that illustrate the focus of the apostles teaching. Sadly, we do not hear much preaching today in this area.

For many Christians, church has been more a place they visit on Sundays (maybe also on Wednesdays) to receive their dose of encouragement and spiritual food for the week. Thus, teachings on living our lives in close relationship with the members of the family of God have not been very relevant.

Instead, in many cases, the focus has been personal: "How can I get what I need from church to survive another week? How can I get wisdom to solve my problems? What are the steps I can take to live a happier more successful life?"

It's that independent mentality that keeps people from seeing themselves as part of a bigger picture. They fail to see themselves as part of the ecclesia, the called out ones with the mission of destroying the works of the devil, setting captives free and establishing the kingdom of God on earth. They have not understood that as they make loving God and loving one another their priority, and as they take their God-given place in His family, they will encounter the loving and all wise Father there!

This change in perspective can only take place as the Holy Spirit begins to reveal to us what God intended all along for His Church on earth, and the important role that love and oneness among His people plays in His purpose, especially in these end times.

The Lord is preparing a people, a Bride, that will be walking in such a deep level of love for Him and forone another that the world will get profound revelations of Jesus. They will actually touch Jesus through them! The lost and the broken will have encounters with the Lord Himself through His people that will bring healing and deliverance for body and soul.

The Lord will manifest His compassion, His mercy, His grace, and His miracle working power through His Church because *"faith* [is] *working through love".* [52]

[52] Gal 5:6 MKJV

SECTION THREE

The Four Keys to Normal Church Life

The Church life is the life of the Body of Jesus Christ. It is about the harmonious cohesiveness of the Church's members. It is about being linked together in unity and love.

Chapter Nine

First key:
A Church that is knit together in Love

It is nearly impossible today for a modern Church to experience the normal Church life that we find in the New Testament.

The obstacle is our modern family paradigm. We are trained by that mindset to live our lives as a nuclear family, independent of other people.

The nuclear family is like an isolated island with very few bridges. On the other hand, the Church family is a Body in which every member is in living, spiritual contact with the other members. We are knit together. As a member in the body of Christ, I am interconnected with every member in that body.

The Church life in the New Testament is not about structure. It's not about how many and what kind of meetings and programs a local church has. The life of the church is the organic life of the Body of Jesus.

My hand has no eyes or mouth, but it is linked and united with my eyes and my mouth. Because of that, my hand can see you and point at you, and you will hear my thumb scream if you hit it with a hammer!

The Body of Christ is linked together in the same way. If I am a finger in that body, I can see and hear the head, **if** my local Church is linked and aligned together with the Prophets.

The reality of the Body life in Christ is that every member in that body is depending on the other members' function. If the eyes are sick and cannot see, the whole body is blind; if the ears are blocked, the lack of hearing will affect all the other members. In addition, if the mouth does not want to eat, weakness becomes the condition of the entire body.

The Church life is an **interdependent** life, which is in contradiction to our modern paradigm in society. Most people want to live an independent life, with little or no accountability to other people. That has also affected many marriages in which couples struggle to melt together. God must work in our lives through wisdom and revelation to change that paradigm.

The Church life in the New Testament is not about structure. It's not about how many and what kind of meetings and programs a local church has. Rather, the life of the Church is the organic life of the Body of Jesus Christ.

It is about the cohesiveness of the Church members' hearts and lives. It is about being linked together in unity and love. It is about functioning together as His *"church, which is His body, the fullness of Him who fills all in all"*. 53

A local Church cannot imitate the normal New Testament Church life; it must be born of the Spirit.

Through Church history many leaders have tried to copy the early Christians' Church life. Some leaders have succeeded in getting their people together every day for meetings. They have also forced their members to sell their possessions and share with the needy. But those leaders have not succeeded in leading their people to experience the dynamic life that the first Church had.

The reason is that the genuine life of the Church must be born of the Spirit.

Christ's Body is a spiritual body. Therefore, the Body life of Jesus in a local church, can only be reproduced in the Spirit where it lives and moves and has its being.

[53] (Ephesians 1:22-23 MKJV)

Paul gives us the key to how we can give birth to the true Church Life.

The key is: *That their hearts might be…knit together in love.*[54]

According to Paul, New Testament Church life has to do with the heart, not structure. The key has nothing to do with how many times we as a Church come together for meetings or any programs we try to add.

The authentic Church Life is something that starts in our hearts. It is all about being knit together in love by a genuine sharing of life's joys, sorrows, struggles and victories.

New Testament Church life has to do with genuine committed relationships, that have as a foundation the love of God and a common passion to honor Him and fulfill His will on this earth.

We can only do this as His sons and daughters in the family of God. These are hearts that have been thoroughly impacted by a revelation from the Father, that becoming one in Him is our grandest destiny and out highest joy!

The Lord Jesus promises us that if we obey His commandment to love one another, our joy will be full! And we all know that the joy of the Lord is our strength! There is no other way to be a strong, courageous people even in the midst of adversity than to abide in His love.

---

[54] Colossians 2:2

The Lord tells us how we can experience joy; *"I have told you this so that you will be as joyful as I am, and your joy will be complete. Love each other as I have loved you. This is what I'm commanding you to do. The greatest love you can show is to give your life for your friends. You are my friends if you obey my commandments...Love each other. This is what I'm commanding you to do."*. [55]

The problem

Because the unity and oneness of the Body of Christ is of such value and importance to God, it stands to reason that it would be a major target of the Enemy. Thus, we can say that without spiritual warfare it will not happen. We must fight for it in the Spirit.

We see this clearly in Colossians 2:1 "*For it is my desire to give you news of the great fight I am making for you and for those at Laodicea, and for all who have not seen my face in the flesh*". [56]

This verse comes before Paul wrote; *That their hearts might be...knit together in love* (V.2).

In verse one Paul stated that he fights a spiritual warfare for the Church in Colosse. He tells us in chapter four, that Epaphras one of his team members "*is always wrestling in his prayers for you*"[57]

[55] Joh 15:11-14, 17 GW

[56] BBE

[57] Colossians 4:12 ISV

Both Paul and his team understood that if the Church in Colosse should come into what God intended for them, it was going to require battling for it in the Spirit.

The spiritual fight was all about hearts being *"knit together in love".*[58]

Anyone that has walked with the Lord for a considerable amount of time and has focused on building relationships, knows from experience that authentic New Testament Church life does not come automatically or cheap. Close relating to our brothers and sisters will often draw out our weaknesses, our insecurities and our vulnerabilities. But if we are willing to pay the price, and fight for it through humility, self-sacrifice and prayer, we will discover the growth of the sweet fragrant fruit of the Spirit in our lives and in the lives of our fellow Christians.

Many have not understood that choosing to stand in love and unity with one another is a form of spiritual warfare because this is what Satan fears more than anything else. A people that have died to their selfish motives and who are determined to walk in love and unity for the sake of Christ are an unstoppable force against the darkness!

By determining to remain humble, to only speak well of one another and to be quick to resolve conflicts, forgiving and forbearing with one another, we are keeping doors shut to the devil.

---

[58] Colossians 2:2

As we all know, the enemy loves to weaken us by causing division and disunity. We must be vigilant not to give him legal access to our churches, for we know that a house divided against itself cannot stand.

The fruit of the warfare

The result of winning this warfare is much more than hearts being knit together. There are wonderful by-products of this oneness! We see this in Colossians 2:2-3; *"Then as their hearts are joined together in love, they will be wonderfully blessed with complete understanding. And they will truly know Christ. Not only is he the key to God's mystery, but all wisdom and knowledge are hidden away in him"*.[59]

Being joined together in the love of God will lead to a corporate revelation and understanding of our Lord Jesus Christ in whom are hidden magnificent secrets of wisdom and knowledge!

The depth of these mysteries can only be unveiled to the Christians who have become one, His Body.

This is what Paul prayed for the Christians in Ephesus; *"I pray that you and all God's holy people will have the power to understand the greatness of Christ's love--how wide, how long, how high, and how deep that love is. Christ's love is greater than anyone can ever know, but I pray that you will be able to know that love. Then you can be filled with everything God has for you".* [60]

---

[59] CEV

[60] Ephesus 3:18-19 ERV

Apostles and prophets have a crucial role to play in the unfolding of the Church's destiny.

Chapter Ten

The second Key: Apostolic Ministry

Many Christians today think that if we are faithful to God and pray, God will take our local church into the authentic Church life that God intended. However, that is not what the New Testament teaches us.

In the Bible we find that certain people in the Body of Christ have received special keys to lead people into their destiny.

Apostle Peter is one of these people. Jesus gave him the keys to the Kingdom[61] and Peter used those keys to

[61] Mathew 16:19

release the Holy Spirit, both to the Jews and to the Samarians as well as to the Gentiles. [62]

Without Peter as an apostle and without his keys, the Samaritans would never have experienced the Kingdom of God and the Holy Spirit.

That is very clear in Act 8:15-17; *"When the two apostles arrived, they prayed that the people would be given the Holy Spirit. Before this, the Holy Spirit had not been given to anyone in Samaria, though some of them had been baptized in the name of the Lord Jesus. Peter and John then placed their hands on everyone who had faith in the Lord, and they were given the Holy Spirit".* [63]

Philip had preached the Gospel for the Samaritans and many had received the Lord as Savior, but none of them had experienced the Holy Spirit. Peter and his ministry as an apostle was the key.

Today, we must understand that without apostles and prophets, the New Testament Church life cannot be established and released. [64]

If we do not receive the apostles and prophets God sends to us and if our local church does not align with them, the Church life that God intended will not become a reality.

It is an error to think that a local church can make it without apostles and prophets.

---

[62] Acts 2:1- 4, 8:14-17, 10:44 - 48

[63] CEV

[64] Ephesus 2:20-22, 3:1-10, 5:32, 1 Corinthians 4:1

Jesus said; *"I will send them prophets and apostles".* [65] The Lord is doing this in our day. He is raising up people that have the keys and the gifts that we need today.

In the New Testament, we find two kinds of Apostles:

1. The twelve apostles of the Lamb [66]

2. Many others are also named as apostles in the New Testament: Paul, Silas, Timothy, Barnabas, Andronicus, Junia, Titus are some of those that have the office of apostle. [67]

There have always been apostles

I believe that the apostolic ministry has always been in the Church through its history. The reformer Luther and the Methodists father, John Wesley are some of the apostles that have taken the Church into a richer manifestation of the Kingdom of God.

Today for an example, David Yongi Cho of South Korea has the largest church in history and has mobilized hundreds of thousands into their callings as pastors, missionaries and intercessors. He is an apostle.

In the 1980's and '90's John Wimber, an apostle and a church planter from California ministered to pastors and

[65] Luke 11:49 KJV
[66] Revelation 21:14
[67] Acts 14:4, Romans 16:7, 2 Corinthians 8:23

impacted hundreds of thousands of Christians in the United States and even internationally by modeling the spreading of the gospel through signs and wonders which he called "power evangelism".

Many others today have been entrusted by God with an apostolic ministry.

The apostolic ministry

The apostolic ministry in the early Church in Jerusalem was the ministry that led the first Christians to encounter the dynamic Church life that we read about in the New Testament. The gift of the pastor or of the teacher alone could never have led the first Christians into that powerful life that we find in the Book of Acts.

Our destiny is in the hands of the people God sends.

It was the Church in Jerusalem that experienced that *"Everyone liked them, and each day the Lord added to.*

"Everyone was amazed by the many miracles and wonders that the apostles worked". [68]

"Having prayed, the place in which they were gathered was shaken, and they were all filled with the Holy Spirit and spoke the Word of God with boldness. And of the multitude of those who believed, the heart and the soul were one". [69]

---

[68] Act 2:43 CEV

[69] Act 4:31-32 LITV

It was the apostles that released this powerful Church life by their teaching and leadership. This apostolic ministry is once again crucial in these last days so that the Church can fulfill her destiny!

Let me define the word Apostle

In Greek, the word is ἀπόστολος – apostolos. Apostle translated in English is the "sent one." In Latin the word is missionary.

This word apostle occurs 81 times in the New Testament. This is an indication of its importance.

Vine's Dictionary tells us that the word apostleship is "a sending, a mission".

An apostle can have various gifts such as teaching, prophecy, or evangelism, but this is not what makes him an apostle.

An apostle is a person sent by God into a situation, city or region for a specific mission or assignment with the authority of Almighty God to accomplish it.

Whereas prophets hear the Lord's direction, apostles have the gift to envision, implement strategies and mobilize people with gifts and callings to fulfill the Lord's will.

The different apostles in the New Testament did not have the same assignment, and they operated out from different gifts.

However, the common thing for all apostles in the New Testament is that they all had the authority of God to establish the scriptural doctrine, advance the Kingdom of God and release the culture of Heaven wherever the Lord sent them with miracles signs and wonders.

Our destiny is in the hands of the people God sends.

Jesus' apostolic ministry [70] was the key for the twelve apostles' destiny.

Paul could never have come into his destiny without God sending Barnabas to take him to Antioch.

It was in that city that God did something very unique. The believers in Antioch *"started to spread the Good News about the Lord Jesus to Greeks...The disciples were called Christians for the first time in the city of Antioch".* [71]

When God sent Barnabas and Paul out as apostles from Antioch they did not just represent what God had done in their personal lives.[72] They also represented the unique work God had done in Antioch.

Wherever they ministered, they gave the people a pure Gospel, not a Gospel just for the Jews, and not a Gospel mingled with the law which was the case in Jerusalem.

---

[70] Hebrew 3:1

[71] Act 11: 20, 26 GW

[72] Acts 13:1-3

Wherever Barnabas and Paul ministered they led the people into their destiny in God through the unique work that God had done in Antioch.

The keys for all of this were the sent ones!

The importance of recognition

The scriptures clearly demonstrate that when people recognize and align with the people that God sends, then we will fulfill our destiny in God.

That message is communicated loud and clear in the book of Ruth. It is amazing to think that a whole book in the Bible is about how a poor Moabite widow, a heathen, recognizes the person that God sends into her life, so that her destiny can be fulfilled: to give birth to the bloodline of Jesus.

Ruth becomes the great grandmother of David. The fruit of her humility and obedience is King David and later God's own Son, the man Christ Jesus. [73]

The simple reason why this amazing thing became a reality is that Ruth gave herself to following Naomi, the person that God had sent into her life.

If we want to fulfill God's destiny for our lives, we must recognize the persons that God sends to us. The Lord is raising up apostles in these days, people who have been proven and tried by Him and persevered through battle. May the Lord give us wisdom and discernment to

---

[73] Ruth 4:17

recognize and align ourselves with those He sends to us.

Jesus never took authority over a person in the Gospels. He took authority over sicknesses and evil spirits, and even over death, but never over a human being.

Chapter Eleven

Align with Apostles

Probably the greatest hindrance for church leaders to embrace the apostolic ministry is the fear of losing control and position in their own local churches.

To come under spiritual authority is a very fearful thing for many Christians. Some have suffered spiritual abuse under leaders who had personal insecurities and hidden agendas.

However, the Bible clearly says to "*obey them that have the rule over you, and submit yourselves*"[74]

By faith we must believe that the Lord has prepared apostles, who out of humble, pure hearts are able to lead His people according to God's will with the fear of the Lord.

[74] Hebrews 13:17

These are people who are broken vessels; they have been tried, tested and purified by God and often endured much suffering through disappointment, betrayal and loss of various kinds. Yet they have emerged as humble bondservants of God, secure and clear concerning their calling, purpose and authority. They are ready to connect and co-labor with other likeminded leaders that have no agenda other than to do the King's will.

Jesus never took authority over a person in the Gospels. He took authority over sicknesses and evil spirits, and even over death, but never over a human being.

Some local church leaders will also fear losing their God-given function if they submit under the spiritual authority of apostles. However, this need not happen if these apostles lead with accountability and with a servant's heart.

Let me illustrate what I am trying to communicate. I am a pastor of a local church. If a mother and father in my church have a problem with their children, I can advise them with wisdom from the scriptures and from the Spirit, but I do not have the right to usurp the parents' authority, by disciplining their children in their own home. If I did that I would be overstepping my sphere of authority and disrespecting theirs.

As a pastor, I need to respect my members' own houses and the authority they have there. In the same way, when they come to the church house, they need to respect the authority that is in that house.

This is my understanding of how apostles should function in their dealings with the different local churches. Their function is to provide servanthood leadership, not to usurp other leaders' authority in their houses.

Apostles must practice the Biblical model of authority.

Jesus never took authority over a person in the Gospels. He took authority over sicknesses and evil spirits, and even over death, but never over a human being.

When the rich young man came to Jesus and asked what he should do to have eternal life. Jesus told him the demands, and he answered, *"I have done this all my life."* Then Jesus said; *"If you want to be perfect, sell what you own. Give the money to the poor, and you will have treasure in heaven. Then follow me! When the young man heard this, he went away sad because he owned a lot of property".* [75]

What is interesting with this story is that Jesus could have commanded the young man to do the right thing, but the Lord let him make his own choice.

What I understand from this story is that authority is not something to be taken by lording it over people, but rather spiritual authority is something to be given to

[75] Matthew 19:21-22 GW

church leaders by the people who trust them and thus are willing to submit to their leadership

Jesus is the Lord but he never demands that place in our lives. It is we who willingly and from our hearts choose to give it when we come to know that He alone is worthy.

As Christians, we should make Jesus the Lord over our finances; but when it comes to giving, He lets us make our own decisions. Paul wrote; *"Each of you should give whatever you have decided. You shouldn't be sorry that you gave or feel forced to give, since God loves a cheerful giver".* [76]

Spiritual authority is a "heart" thing. God doesn't want obedience by coercion. He wants us to submit to His authority willingly because we love Him. We see this very clearly from Philippians 2:13; *"For it is God who is producing in you both the desire and the ability to do what pleases him".* [77]

Our view of Church determines our leadership style.

A Christian leader's view of the Church will determine how he deals with his church's members. If he doesn't understand that the Church is his extended family, he will not see his role in his church as a spiritual father.

---

[76] 2 Corinthians 9:7 GW

[77] ISV

Furthermore, he will probably see his staff as employees rather than brothers and sisters to whom he is committed.

The archetype of leadership in the Bible is God's spiritual Fatherhood. It is a Father who is the leader in heaven and on the earth. [78]

God wants spiritual fathers to lead his Church. Paul said; *"For though you have ten thousand instructors in Christ, yet you do not have many fathers".* [79]

To lead a local Church is to lead an extended family and therefore, the ability to be a spiritual father is of utmost importance. That is why the leaders in the local church in the New Testament are called elders.[80] That title indicates maturity and age and fatherhood, not specific gifts.

However, some elders did have a gift of teaching. Others had a shepherd or prophetic gift and some of the elders were simply mature Christians of excellent character who lived out the life of Christ in a way that others could imitate. [81]

The latter elders were pillars in the local temple of God even though they may have been men of few words. A pillar does not speak, but they nevertheless hold up the temple. A heavy spiritual weight is on theirshoulders.

---

[78] Matheus 6:9, Ephesus 3:14-15
[79] 1Corinthens 4:15 MKJV
[80] Acts 14:23; Titus 1:5
[81] 1 Corinthians 4:16

Professional clergy does not represent Biblical, apostolic Christianity.

Some pastors, prophets, apostles and other ministries are often placed on a pedestal. That becomes a temptation for some leaders. They begin to think that they are superior above other "ordinary" men and women in church.

Thankfully, most pastors and ministries that I know do not have this attitude. They want with their whole heart to serve the Lord and His people. They are honest and want to do the will of God. They do not lord it over their people but rather they are faithful servant leaders.

However, some pastors and ministry leaders see their position as one of power. They are in control. They are the "head honcho". They have the title, the position and they are the only ones that lead and preach every Sunday and their people idolize them.

They love it when their people put them on a pedestal. Because of this, those gifted and successful pastors and leaders begin in their heart to gradually develop a sense of entitlement and self-satisfaction. Pride has begun to enter their hearts.

After a year or two, those pastors and leaders begin to see themselves above everyone else. Slowly new attitudes begin to manifest towards their congregation. Now they are disrespectful, condescending and arrogant in their dealings with their people. They are also more vulnerable to a moral failure because of lack of accountability.

This is obviously a killer for the atmosphere of mutual love, respect and care that God wants for the Body of Christ in a local church. Instead, it produces a dysfunctional family where the father is abusive and people are co-dependent and controlled by fear and intimidation.

How can a church/ministry protect the pastor/leader?

1. **Leadership in the New Testament is always plural.** No church/ministry in the New Testament had just one leader. Multiple leaders, therefore, will serve as a "check and balance" and serve as a safeguard against the human tendency to play God over other people.

2. **Create a system of pastoral accountability.** This allows for people toappeal to an authority outside the local church. Ask outside pastors, prophets, apostles and other leaders to be the mediators in a crises situation or be a part of the board. This creates a system where grievances can be investigated and acted on by fellow ministers in an objective way.

3. **Create a system of financial accountability.** "Open the books". Not only

> for gross revenue and expenditures, but also in matters of reimbursement. There is no excuse and no reason that this information can't be public to church members and givers.

To summarize, because the Church is first and foremost a family, then apostles, pastors and all leaders must lead with the heart of the Heavenly Father. Their aim and their desire should be to build up their sons and daughters and see them come into their purpose and destinies in Christ. This should be a great joy for them even if it means that some sons and daughters surpass their father's anointing and influence.

If we desire to have the same dynamic life that the first Church had, we must be committed to imitating their lifestyle.

Chapter Twelve

The Third Key: Imitate the first Church

"And they continued steadfastly in the apostles' doctrine and fellowship, and in breaking of bread, and in prayers.". [82]

The first Church in Jerusalem expressed its Church life in four different ways:

1. *"They continued steadfastly in the apostles Doctrine"*

2. *"and fellowshipped"* with the Lord and with each other

[82] Act 2:42

3. *“and in prayers”*

4. *“and in breaking bread”* daily in their homes (The Lord’s Supper).

If we desire to have the same dynamic life that the first Church had, we must be committed to imitating their lifestyle.

However, let me give a warning: the first Church’s lifestyle must be born through the Holy Spirit and prayer. We cannot produce it or contrive it through our own effort and power.

The apostles' doctrine

The first Church did not just listen and agree with the apostles’ doctrine. They committed themselves to steadfastly obeying their teaching.

The teaching of doctrine is different from preaching.[83] Preaching is to give spiritual food in order to exhort, strengthen, comfort and encourage people in the Lord.

It is like prophesying. Paul tells us; *“He who prophesies speaks to men for building up, and exhortation, and comfort”.* [84]

In John 6:63 Jesus said; *“The words that I speak toyou are spirit and are life”.*[85] That is what preaching isall

[83] 2 Timotheus 1:11
[84] 1Co 14:3 MKJV
[85] MKJV

about. It carries the life and the Spirit of God. The target is mainly the heart not the mind, although understanding will also come with it.

The teaching of doctrine when done with God-given anointing and authority will give knowledge and understanding and establish believers in obedience to the Word of God.

The apostles' doctrine targets the mind and the understanding, and when it is received with the fear of the Lord, the will is conformed to His will. Doctrine when taught with God-given authority will reach our hearts and feet so that we walk in the *"obedience to the faith"*.[86]

The doctrine of the apostles lays a Biblical foundation for the Kingdom of God and its culture in the Church.[87]

We have the apostles' doctrine in the New Testament. However, a lot of that doctrine is still hidden as secrets in the pages of the New Testament. It takes an apostle to unlock the secrets of the Church in the New Testament.[88]

The Eucharist

The expression, *"breaking bread"*, in Acts 2:42 is an expression for the Lord's supper – the Eucharist.

---

[86](Rom 1:5

[87] Ephesians 2:20, 1 Corinthians 3:10-12

[88] Ephesians 3:1-9, 5:32, 1 Corinthians 4:1

As you recall, Jesus introduced His supper in the context of a Passover meal in a home. That is why we read in the book of Acts; *"They broke bread together in different homes and shared their food happily and freely".*[89]

Today, many churches take the Lord's supper only once a month. The first Christians did it every day with a meal. The reason they did it every day is that the Lord's supper was part of their spiritual warfare.

Paul tells us, *"For as often as you may eat this bread, and drink this cup, you solemnly proclaim the death of the Lord, until He shall come".* [90]

The Lord's supper is a warfare decree against the enemy. The Lord's supper is proclaiming the death of Jesus, the shedding of His blood, and His mighty victory over the enemy. The target is the evil spirits in the unseen world.

The Lord's supper is a mighty weapon. We should use it as often as it is practical for us to do so. It is a powerful thing to do as married couples in our homes as we pray for our families.

Praise and worship and the Word of God are among our mightiest weapons as children of God. When we then add the Lord's supper to our arsenal which proclaims Jesus's total and irreversible victory over Satan, sin and death by His shed blood we are capable of doing great

[89] Act 2:46 CEV

[90] 1Co 11:26 LITV

damage to the Enemy's agenda. I believe this is why our Lord gave His people this command the night before He was betrayed.

To eat and drink of the body and the blood of Jesus Christ is a prophetic act that releases the power of God against Satan and his schemes.

The power in the Lord's Supper

Because the Lord's supper is so powerful, the scriptures warn us against partaking in an unworthy manner. Doing so can lead to sickness and even death.

The Lord's supper is a mighty weapon. We should use it so often it is practical for us today.

Paul tells us that[91]; *"If you eat the bread and drink the wine in a way that isn't worthy of the Lord, you sin against his body and blood. That's why you must examine the way you eat and drink. If you fail to understand that you are the body of the Lord, you will condemn yourselves by the way you eat and drink. That's why many of you are sick and weak and why a lot of others have died".* [92]

The Lord's supper; spiritual realities!

[91] 1 Corinthians 11:27-30 CEV

The power in the Lord's supper lies in the Bread and Wine. In my understanding they are not just symbols; they are powerful spiritual realities.

Jesus said very clearly about the Bread *"this is my body"*[93] and about the Wine *"this is my blood"*.

Our heavenly reality is this: when we partake of the physical bread and wine here on the earth by faith, we enter the Holy of Holies in heaven and there we partake of the eternal body of Christ and of His eternal blood.

As Christians, we are standing on this earth with our two feet, but at the same time we are also through our spirit living in heaven. Paul tells us this; *"God raised us from death and seated us together with him in the heavenly places"*. [94]

The message of the communion table; we are one powerful family under the Lord Jesus Christ

When we then look at the Lord's Supper as a mighty spiritual weapon in the context of the corporate family of God, we can see the powerful spiritual ramifications of a united Church that partakes together in covenant love, commitment, unity, holiness and in unreserved surrender to the will of the King.

There is a unique bond that takes place when God's people share the communion table with understanding

---

[93] Mat 26:26-28

[94] Ephesus 2:6 ERV

and in the love and peace of God which shuts out the Enemy.

Paul confirms this for us in 1Co 10:16; *"When we drink from the cup that we ask God to bless, isn't that sharing in the blood of Christ? When we eat the bread that we break, isn't that sharing in the body of Christ"*? [95]

The act of partaking of the body and blood of Jesus Christ in one accord, has the immeasurable potential of proclaiming the victory of the blood shed on the cross of Calvary that shakes the kingdom of darkness and disarms the Enemy in a local church, a city or a region!

This is an important secret that the first Christians had. This secret is one of the keys that enabled them to experience the genuine, dynamic Church life that we read about in the New Testament.

[95] CEV

The first Christians had their brethren in their homes on a regular basic. Hospitality was a normal part of their Church life.

Chapter Thirteen

The Fourth Key: Understanding the Word Fellowship

"And they continued steadfastly in the… fellowship" [96]

The early Christians had their brothers and sisters in their homes on a regular basis. Hospitality was a normal part of their Church life.

[96] Act 2:42 KJV

Hospitality

Did you know that the Bible speaks strongly about hospitality and exhorts us to invite brothers and sisters into our home and share our daily bread with them?

This is the teaching of the New Testament:

"Be hospitable to one another without murmurings". [97]

"Always practice hospitality". [98]

"An elder must be ready to help people by welcoming them into his home". [99]

"Don't forget to show hospitality to believers you don't know. By doing this some believers have shown hospitality to angels without being aware of it". [100]

The biggest thing in the first church was not meetings; it was the fellowship with God and with one another. The early Christians met every day for fellowship in their homes.

The most important thing in a modern Church is the Sunday morning service, and the most important thing in that service is the senior pastor's sermon.

In the early Church, the apostles' teaching was important, but of utmost importance in their Church life

---

[97] 1Peter 4:9 KJV
[98] Romans 12:13 WNT
[99] Titus1:8 ERV
[100] Hebrew 13:2 GW

was the **fellowship** which in Greek it's called **koinonia**. This went far beyond socializing. It was the sharing of their lives together and took more of their time than anything else.

The biblical New Testament understanding of the word fellowship entails a much deeper level of openness than we encounter in the typical modern church.

> **God wants radical transparency. That means I do not try to hide myself behind a mask. I have taken off my mask and what you see is who I am.**

Psalms 42:7 gives us a glimpse of God's heart: *"Deep calls to deep"*. That expression describes our deep heart to heart and spirit to Spirit fellowship with God.

The koinonia shared by the early Christians had this quality about it. It was the depth in their spirit that called for the depth in their brother's spirit, and they shared those deep things with each other and with the Lord. [101]

Walking in the light

I believe that the words in 1John 1:7 has hidden secrets about the early Christian's koinonia. If we delve into that verse, then it is possible for us to understand the Greek word koinonia in a deeper way.

John wrote; *"But if we walk in the light, as he is in the light, we have fellowship one with another, and the*

[101] 1 John 1:3

blood of Jesus Christ his Son cleanseth us from all sin". 102

My understanding of this verse is this:

First: Apostle John commands members in the Church to *"walk in the light".*

Second: The expression; *"if we walk in the light, as he is in the light",* does not point to our individual walk with God. The word *"we"* means you and I, and everyone in the Body of Christ.

Third: The Church should walk in a special way. Our walk with each other should be *"in the light."*

What does that mean?

The walk in the light causes us to open up the "curtains" in our lives. That means I can see into your life and you can see into my life. No closed curtains. That is a walk in the light.

Many times when people come to the Church they have "the Church mask" on. They hide behind that mask. They tell people how wonderful everything is. They praise God, but inside they are hurting and in distress. They are afraid to be honest for fear of being judged or rejected, so they do not tell how things really are and do not practice open and straight communication.

[102] 1John 1:7 MKJV

God wants radical transparency. That means I do not try to hide myself behind a mask. I have taken off my mask, and what you see is who I am.

The **koinonia** that God wants is the unmasked fellowship with no hidden agenda.

Radical openness with one another is the way into the normal, genuine dynamic Church Life.

It must be stated that you cannot and should not be expected to do this with everybody. Nevertheless, if you want to experience New Testament Church life, you need a small group of church friends whom you can trust and with whom you can walk in the light. That is why cell groups in a local Church are so important; that is one place where people can get to know one another more intimately and have the courage to share their lives with one another. It also serves as protection because of the accountability that it provides.

The blessings of walking in the light

"But if we walk in the light, as he is in the light, we have fellowship one with another, and the blood of Jesus Christ his Son cleanseth us from all sin". [103]

Transparency and open honest communication leads us into wonderful blessings.

[103] 1John 1:7MKJV

The first thing that happens when we walk in the light with other Christians; is that "*we have fellowship one with another*".

The reality of Biblical fellowship - Koinonia is not possible without walking in the light.

The second thing that we experience when we walk in the light is *"the blood of Jesus Christ his Son cleanseth us from all sin"*.

"Light walking" with other Christians will not only bring forgiveness into our lives, but will also assure us that, *"the blood sacrifice of Jesus, God's Son, washes away every sin and makes us clean"*. [104]

Forgiveness is one thing; purification is another. Both of those realities will be released to us when radical transparency comes into our Church relationships.

The koinonia of the first Christians was the quality of life that allowed them to experience the fullness and the richness of the life of God Himself.

Apostle John wrote; "*that which we have seen and heard we declare to you, that you also may have fellowship with us; and truly our fellowship is with the*

Father and with His Son Jesus Christ. And these things we write to you that your joy may be full".[105]

[104] 1John 1:7 ERV
[105] John 1:3-4

SECTION FOUR

Deeper Revelation

The Church is organic because the Church is not a nonprofit organization or an institution. It is a living thing.

Chapter Fourteen

The Organic Church

"The church, which is His body,
the fullness of Him who fills all in all". [106]

The body of Christ is an organic spiritual reality.

The Church is organic because it is not a nonprofit organization nor an institution. It is a living thing.

The body of Christ is made up of two living elements. One is Jesus Christ and the other is the people that have been called out from the secular society to be the Body of Christ, the **ecclesia.** When these two spiritual living organic elements come together, then you have the reality of the word "Church".

[106] Ephesus 1:22-23 MKJV

Paul's understanding of Christ's Body on earth

"In him all the parts of the building fit together and grow into a holy temple in the Lord. Through him you, also, are being built in the Spirit together with others into a place where God lives". [107]

Paul tells us that the Church grows into a holy temple. The word *"grow"* is an organic word since only living things grow. Again, the Church is a living spiritual Body.

"fit together"

The Greek words for *"fit together"* means to sew together; to unite; to make one.

Paul understood that Christ alone knows how to position each member in His Body where it belongs and that the different members are meant to be united together. Because they are all a part of the same Body, they are created to relate to one another in a good organic way.

The reason for this is according to Paul; *"God has put the body together".* [108]

The foot is in its right place; it should not be where the head or the hand is. The eye is in its proper place; it should not be in the knee or the heel. The mouth, the tongue, the teeth, the lungs, the heart, are in their proper places. They are all where God placed them.

[107] Ephesus 2:21-22 GW
[108] 1 Corinthians 12:24 ISV

What are the practical ramifications?

A good example of the members of the Body functioning organically together is what happened on the first Day of Pentecost.

Act 2:14 tells us that *"Peter, standing up with the Eleven, lifted up his voice and said....".* [109]

Peter's message that day brought 3000 Jews into the Kingdom of God.

The way a finger finds its place is to look around to see where it is located. When the finger sees the other fingers on the hand, it understands its place and function.

Why is it that Peter is the one that delivered the preaching that day? Had the twelve organized themselves and appointed Peter as the senior apostle? We find nothing in the Book of Acts that points to that.

What we see is that the twelve apostles had been walking together for more than three years. During that time, they did not only learn to relate to one another in a right way, they also got to know the gifting and the authority of the others.

Therefore, they could show deference to Peter and allow him to be the spokesman because they acknowledged who he was in God.

[109] MKJV

It was very natural for the twelve to give room for Peter to deliver the message on the Day of Pentecost without dispute or competition. Furthermore, Peter is the one that God gave the message to.

Relating and functioning organically in the Spirit, comes through recognition.

We see this clearly in Acts 13. In the beginning of that chapter, the Church in Antioch sends out Barnabas and Saul as apostles.

Barnabas is the leader and his name comes before Saul's in verse 2 and 7. However, interestingly, this changes after Saul (also called Paul) authoritatively deals with Elymas, the sorcerer, who opposed them. Thereafter, he is called Paul and he is now the leader in verse 13.

Luke, the author of Acts, recognizes this leadership shift in the apostolic team. He now places Paul's name before Barnabas in verse 46.

What is interesting with these facts is this:

1. Neither Paul nor Barnabas fight for their position.
2. They did not try to create an order with human understanding.
3. They related to each other in a spiritual and organic way. They recognized God's will.

4. Barnabas began as the team leader but God changed that. Barnabas recognized this without a power struggle. That is maturity.

God chose your place in the Body of Christ.

The first Church did not organize people with human understanding and place them at will in different positions.

The only organizing that the first Church did was forthe daily distribution of food. The Church members chose the men that should do that practical work.

The first Church recognized the will of God, the gifts He had given, and then gave the person room to function.[110] This is what God wants today in His Church.

An excellent example of this truth is Claire, a woman in her early 70's who has become a member of our local church this year. She is Spirit-filled and has walked with the Lord for almost 40 years. Claire is a classicfive-fold evangelist with an amazing gift for reaching out to people with the love of God in restaurants, in stores, at the doctor's office and anywhere else she goes. The joy and compassion of God radiates from her and she flows beautifully with the word of knowledge which God uses to open the hearts of the people shetouches.

She has written her testimony in a beautifully done pamphlet with her picture on the front. It also includes

---

[110] 1 Corinthians 12:28, Acts 1:15-26

the basic gospel message with scriptures, the prayer of salvation and her personal contact information. Claire has also equipped other Christians to do the same.

Yet, although this woman of God is spiritually mature and uniquely gifted and anointed to do the work of an evangelist and to equip others, she has gone from church to church and never been truly acknowledged and affirmed for who she is. Only now does she feel she has landed where she has connected heart to heart and spirit to spirit with like-minded fellow leaders. Claire has begun a new season with the Lord in which she will launch out to impart her passion and equip the saints for the work of the ministry in a way she has never done before.

How a finger finds it's place and functions.

If we use the hand as a metaphor, we can say that a finger finds its place by looking around to see where it is located. When the finger sees the other fingers on the hand, its understands its place and function.

Paul tells us; *"But now God has set the members, each one of them, in the body as it has pleased Him."*. [111]

But it is one thing to know your place in the Body and another thing to learn to work together with the other members of Christ's Body.

[111] 1Co 12:18 MKJV

As a child, it took a few years for my physical fingers to learn to harmonize and become an effective hand receiving direction from my brain in my head.

Just now, my hands express the message God has given me, by writing this book. My heart and mind have received the word, but because my fingers have learned to harmonize, my hands can write the word of God on my computer.

You find your ministry the same way as a finger on the hand; you need to understand your particular gifts as well as where and with whom God has place you.

Just as the five fingers of the hand work together to receive direction from the head to be its effective expression, your purpose and calling will complement and harmonize with that of the brothers and sisters with whom God connects you. As you learn to work "as one hand", the will of your Head, Jesus Christ, will be manifested.

In the same way, Jesus, the Head is using you and everyone else in the Body of Christ, *"so that through the church the manifold wisdom of God might now be made known to the rulers and authorities in the heavenly places".* [112]

Once again, we see that discovering and gratefully accepting our place in the organic Body of Christ and functioning in it in harmony with our brethren, speaks

---

[112] Ephesians 3:10 ESV

something loud and clear to the rulers and authorities in the heavenly places. Why? Because when they see the united Church they see Jesus Himself and tremble!

If we are spiritual plants, then we hurt ourselves if we do not remain in the place where God has planted us.

Chapter Fifteen

Relationships in the Body of Christ

Next time you sit in your local church, look around to the right and to the left, to the back and in front of you. If you have been led by the Spirit to that body of people, what you see is your extended family.

You did not choose everyone in your church family, but it is not an accident that you are a part of this extended family that you now see. God, in His love, has placed you there. What you see all around you are your sisters and your brothers, your spiritual fathers and your spiritual mothers and maybe even your spiritual sons and daughters.

When it comes to your biological father and mother or your biological sisters and brothers, you did not choose them either. God made that choice for you.

Your relationships with your biological family are not just for a short time. Those relationships are intended to endure until death do you part.

In a similar way, this is also God's intention with our relationships in the Church. To move from church to church is not the perfect will of God, although we all know that sometimes our journey takes us through various stages until we finally come home.

The Bible speaks about; *"Those that are planted in the house of the LORD shall flourish in the courts of our God".* [113]

If we are spiritual plants, then we hurt ourselves if we do not remain in the place where God has planted us. Common sense tells us that no plant can flourish and blossom if you transplant it time after time.

God wants Close Covenant Relationships

[113] Psalm 92:13 JUB

Paul tells us how close God wants our relationships to be in Ephesians 2:21-22; *"In whom all the building fitly framed together groweth unto an holy temple in the*

Lord: In whom ye also are builded together for an habitation of God through the Spirit".

It is very clear here that the purpose of God is that the Church should become a temple, a dwelling place, for the presence of God. That happens through a building and growth process.

God does not want a pile of living stones no matter how big that pile is. He wants a home – a spiritual house - where the presence of God is manifested.

Paul speaks about the building process. He speaks of our reality, namely, that we are a part of God's temple.
We are stones that are fit together with others. We *"are builded together"* and we are *"fitly framed together".*

Paul is not speaking about bricks that are made by human hands. He is talking about stones like those found in nature.

The expression *"fitly framed together"* communicates that God, like the stone builders in the old days, searches for stones that can fit together and then places them together.

In other words, God has put you together with people that are fit for you. Because of that, you can have togetherness and close relationship with those stones –

the people that are placed by God around you. You are *"fitly framed together"* with them. Your gifting and personality will complement and fit together with the other stones to walk in prepared works and glorify God.

Peter's Messages

The Apostle Peter tells us also about this building process: *"you, too, as living stones, are building yourselves up into a spiritual house".* [114]

God does not want a pile of living stones no matter how many or how lively they are! He wants a home, **a spiritual house**, where He can dwell and manifest His presence.

The local church is a place for building the temple of God. In other words, God does not want people just to come to a place of worship for some praise and worship music and a preaching.

He wants a people who understand what it means to be His family, His Body and who whole-heartedly commit themselves to loving one another with the love of God and to iron out differences in a righteous way by applying God's principles.

He wants everyone to be intentional about relationship building because they truly love the Lord and they want to see the desire of His heart be fulfilled.

[114] 1 Peter 2:5 ISV

For the Church to be a house that manifest the presence of God it must become a place for "Body Building". It is only through building relationships, that the Church will come into its true and full destiny.

To build that house for God means that I allow God to place stones all around me: over me, under me, in front of me, in back of me and on each side of me. That means intimate and transparent relationships.

"Sandpaper ministry"

We need to be realistic about the normal Church life. This life entails self-sacrifice and the willingness to apply the Word of God to our relationships. When people live in close relationships, a certain amount of conflict is inevitable. Family life is wonderful, but not without a price and not without calling upon the wisdom from above to navigate through conflict resolution.

The Apostle James tells us; "*But the wisdom from above is first pure, then peaceable, gentle,* ***willing to yield****, full of mercy and good fruits, without partiality and without hypocrisy*"[115].

We find few local churches that live this radical commitment among its members. Thus, the normal New Testament Church life is abnormal for the common "normal" local church.

Paul is very realistic in his teaching about Church life. He tells us that we will experience hurts and conflicts in

[115] James 3:17 EMTV

our relationships with other brothers and sisters. However, he also exhorts how we should respond: *"forbearing one another, and forgiving each other, if any man have a complaint against any; even as the Lord forgave you, so also do ye".* [116]

What I call the "sandpaper" ministry will be a reality in the normal New Testament Church life. Every living stone will experience how its rough edges get smoothed down by relating to the other living stones with whom they share life.

Some situations may actually be quite intense and painful, but just as in a marriage the thought of "divorce" is not an (easy) option. The Lord uses these situations to purify our hearts if we humble ourselves before Him.

As God's sons and daughters, we must resolve to do everything to restore and build our relationships by God's grace. After all, Jesus clearly stated that it is our genuine love for one another that will be our most powerful witness to a lost and broken world.[117]

The Apostle Paul tells us in the following truth: *"Love is more important than anything else. It is what ties everything completely together".* [118]

In other words, love is the cement that keeps the stones together. The need of "love-cement" cannot be over emphasized in a local Church.

---

[116] Colossians 3:13 ASV
[117] John 13:35
[118] Colossians 3:14 CEV

When "the love-cement" is between the stones, the devil may try to pull one out but he will not succeed. Furthermore, "the love-cement" is a powerful protection against Church divisions and splits.

The importance of closely relating to the right people

Let me illustrate this. Say that you live in a room that has only one door. And you cannot walk out through that door. Every one that comes into your room comes to stay there with you for the rest of your life because there is no exit door. That means that for the remainder of your life you will live with the people that are in your room.

The people in your room will impact the quality of your life – for better or for worse. Your happiness depends on who is in your room and is determined by how you can relate to them.

Let me now reveal the truth about this illustration; this room that has no exit door is your family that you are born into.

There is no way out from your family. Your happiness and quality of life, especially in your childhood and youth depend on who is in your family and how you can relate to them.

However, although it may come as a shock for most people, the room without an exit door is also true about the Church. The Church family is not meant to have an exit door. Some Christians have made it easy to exit, but God never put an exit door in the Church.

The Lord is very serious about covenant and faithfulness. This is why it is so important that we are led by God when committing ourselves to a church family. Although the Lord will sometimes lead people to relocate to another local church for various reasons, the sad fact is that many choose to leave without God's blessing.

"The Body-of-Christ reality"

As difficult as it may sound, the only thing you can do with this fact, is to surrender to it and trust that God never demands something out from us that He does not equip us with the grace to obey. There is no way out from this "Body-of-Christ reality"!

The people that God in His love has placed you together with perhaps may not look like you or function like you, but the Lord has a perfect plan for how you can work in harmony.

That is what Paul tells us; *"In him all the parts of the building fit together".*[119]

You and the people around you in your local Body are created by God to function together in an organic way as each member discovers their purpose and is released into it.

---

[119] Ephesus 2:21-22 GW

For the Church to become not just a light but the light for the whole world around it, it must be a Citywide Church.

Chapter Sixteen

The Unity of the Church

In Matthew chapter five, Jesus gives the revelation that the Church is a *"city"*.

Jesus said, *"You are the light of the world. A city that is set on a hill cannot be hidden"*. [120]

In a city you have many houses that light up the world around it. As you look down during a night flight, you know that one house cannot light up an entire city; you need many houses both large and small to be simultaneously radiating their light.

---

[120] Matthew5:14

One local church is not enough for giving light to a whole city. All the churches and ministries in a city need to be built together to be the light that God intended for the world in and around the city.

In the letter to the citywide Church in Ephesus, Paul stresses the importance of being built together into a "City Temple". *"In him all the parts of the building fit together and grow into a holy temple in the Lord".* [121]

For the Church to become not just a light but the light for the whole world around it, it must be a Citywide Church.

A Citywide Church is the place where gifts and resources from the local churches connect to produce a synergy for a fuller manifestation of the light of Christ.

The Citywide Church

Why is it that the only names for local churches in the New Testament are names of cities such as the Church in Rome, in Corinth, in Thessalonica and in Ephesus?

Could it be that the only way Heaven can be expressed here on this earth in its fullness is through Citywide Churches?

What do I mean by the term Citywide Church?

[121] Ephesus 2:21, GW

In the New Testament we do not find anything comparable to our modern local churches. Actually, there were no church buildings before 300 A.D.

The believers in the New Testament gathered together in house churches. [122]

These house churches saw themselves as being part of a Citywide Church.

The Church in Corinth was one such Citywide Church. The Amplified Bible expresses this very clearly in 1 Corinthians 3:16; *"Do you not discern and understand that you* [the whole church at Corinth] *are God's temple (His sanctuary), and that God's Spirit has His permanent dwelling in you* [to be at home in you, collectively as a church and also individually]"?

Ancient Rome was the largest city in the then known world. At the time of Paul, it took a person one whole day to go from one end of the city to the other. Nevertheless, in New Testament times, the Church in Rome was considered to be one entity, a Citywide Church.

How was the New Testament Citywide Church able to function as one entity? The answer is: there were persons that functioned as connectors just as the joints do in our physical body.[123]

---

[122] Romans 16:5, 1 Corinthians 15:19, Colossians 4:15, Philemon 1:2

[123] See Colossians 2:19

These joints were the elders in the Church. The elders were not just overseers over a house church; they were overseers over a Citywide Church.

The concept of a Citywide Church does not mean that every local church and ministry must come under the same legal umbrella.

Although God has only one Church in a city, the Body of Christ, that Church is made up of many congregations and ministries.

The Church of God in a city is not a legal entity or a Christian association. According to Paul the Citywide Church is a spiritual organism, *"the church, which is His body".*[124]

The Citywide Church consists of genuine, purposeful relationships as Paul points out in Ephesians 2:22. *"You... are built together for a dwelling place of God through the Spirit".*

For a Citywide Church to be built together it is not necessary for denominational churches and individual Christians to leave their commitment to their local churches and denominations, although God may sometimes lead in this way.

However, they do need to practice Paul's teaching in Romans 15:7; *"Receive one another as Christ also received us, to the glory of God."*

---

[124] Ephesians 1:22-23

The basis upon which Christ receives us is not that we have given mental assent to the right doctrine. It is by

grace through faith in His cross and resurrection that we receive the life of God. This is also the basis upon which we must receive one another. Anyone who has the Spirit of God through genuine faith in Jesus Christ is my brother or my sister.

I want to have as many brothers and sisters, as belong to the household of God. Because of that, I accept all my born-again brothers and sisters regardless of church affiliation as long as we are not compromising the fundamental tenets of our Christian faith.

I am a strong believer in the concept of the citywide Church because it takes a strong representation of unity across denominational and racial lines for the city to express heaven in a city in such a way that the enemy's power is broken and the spiritual atmosphere is changed.

The twelve tribes of Israel carry a message.

Israel was one nation with twelve different tribes; each tribe had a different calling and function.

One of the lessons that the people of God who came out from Egypt learned in the wilderness, was that they must march together and function in unity to take the promise land and manifest the Kingdom of God in that geographic area.

The Citywide Church is made up of many tribes (denominations and spiritual streams). The day when the Citywide Church begins to march and function together as one Church, will be the day of revival and of the manifestation of the Kingdom of God in that city's geographic area.

That was what Jesus prayed for; *"I pray that all of these people continue to have unity in the way that you, Father, are in me and I am in you. I pray that they may be united with us so that the worldwill believe that you have sent me".*[125]

The Citywide Church contains a unity of diversity, not a unity of conformity.

God wants the diversity that exists in the present-day Church. He has given the local Churches and ministries various callings and giftings. That is one of the reasons why we have different streams in the body of Christ.

Another reason is that we, as an individual church, are limited in our soul's capacity to receive and manifest everything God is, has and can.

A third reason for diverse streams in the body of Christ is that local Churches on this earth have received different revelations of Jesus.

[125] Joh 17:21 GW

The Churches in Revelation are given different revelations of Jesus.

In the book of Revelation, we find that every one of the seven churches in chapter two and three has a different revelation of Jesus. Because of that they manifest Jesus in different ways.

"To the church in Ephesus, write:
The one who holds the seven stars in his right hand, the one who walks among the seven gold lamp stands, says….".[126]

"The church in Pergamum, write: *The one who holds the sharp two-edged sword says..."*.[127]

"The church in Thyatira, write: *The Son of God, whose eyes are like flames of fire and whose feet are like glowing bronze, says…"*.[128]

All seven Churches in Revelation chapter two and three are given a different part of the revelation of Jesus that John sees in the first chapter. They each receive something totally unique.

God is still doing this in present-day local churches. These different revelations are meant to enrich the Body of Christ as a whole, and not to cause division. This is

---

[126] Rev 2:1 GW
[127] Rev 2:12 GW
[128] Rev 2:18 GW

also the reason for the different streams in the Body of Christ today.

The Problem

There are approximately 41,000 Christian denominations on this earth, according to the center for the study of Global Christianity.

Throughout Church history we have seen how new denominations have been formed as a result of disagreement and difficult divisions.

It is a sad reality that many local churches compete with one another instead of marching together and functioning in unity. They build their own "kingdom".

When the physical body turns on itself, we have a problem. The name of the problem is cancer.

Cancer is a reality when cells grow without regard to the rest of the body. Self-centered congregations that promote their own growth without regard to the Citywide Church are like a cancer growing in the body of Christ.

A healthy body has organs that do not compete with each other. The body needs all of its organs such as the heart, the lungs, the stomach, the kidneys and all the other organs to work together in harmony for good health. In the same way, the Body of Christ needs all the different local churches to be in harmony with each other in order to overcome the conflicts and severe challenges that are coming at the end of this age.

An independent local church will not be able to withstand the increased pressures and the conflicts that are certain to come in the not too distant future.

It was said before the civil war, to the original thirteen American colonies that they must "Join or die".

That is the choice today for many local churches.

The age of the church as we've known it is drawing to an end. Today the apostolic church is dawning.

Chapter Seventeen

How Do We Handle the New Thing God is doing?

The age of church as usual is drawing to an end. Today the apostolic church is dawning. It is a church of great outpouring of miracles, signs and wonders and of great harvest. It is AD 30 all over again but with much greater access to revelation of our inheritance and of our calling as the end-times ecclesia. We are now living in the midst of epic changes.

Today millions of Christians have been led to redefine Church

In the past the established Protestant churches have persecuted or at best rejected any new movement or alternative church structure.

The Catholic Church has handled that situation differently. Nearly every renewal movement has been embraced by the official church and allowed to build up a new structure outside the established church structure.

An example is the Catholic Charismatic movement which was born by the Spirit of God in February 1967 on a retreat held by several faculty members and students from the Catholic Duquesne University. This group gathered to seek God and to their amazement received their own Pentecost as the Holy Spirit fell on them with the manifestations of tongues and prophecy. This was the birth of a whole new revelation of Jesus and of the power of the Holy Spirit for evangelism, healing, deliverance and for living the Christian life in victory.

Today you find Charismatic Catholics in 230 countries, and as of 2003 there were 119 million Catholics active in the movement according to David Barret, Global Evangelization. There are presumably more countries impacted today and millions more Spirit-filled Catholics in 2016.

Three popes have acknowledged the movement: Pope Paul VI, Pope John Paul II, and Pope Benedict XVI.

The Catholic Church has handled the Charismatics in a totally different way than many denominations in the United States.

What is the Biblical way to handle this redefining that the Church is facing?

Jesus shows us the way: *"No one puts a piece of a new garment on an old garment. Otherwise, both the new will tear, and the old does not match the piece from the new. And no one puts new wine into old wineskins. Else the new wine will burst the wineskins and be spilled, and the wineskin will perish. But new wine must be put intonew wineskins, and both are preserved together. Also no one having drunk old wine immediately desires new, for he says, The old is better.*[129]

In my understanding, the new wineskin and the old wineskin speaks about church structure.

Jesus is saying here that God cares about and wants to preserve both the old wineskin as well as the new because He cares about the people that are in them. However, if you put the old and the new structures together, both will be destroyed. Leaders need humility to accept this reality.

God wants to preserve the main line churches!

The establishment must give freedom to new structures in the same way that a father and mother let their children establish new homes. At the same time the old and the new need to work on their relationship and be

---

[129] Luke. 5:36-39

"eager to keep the unity of the Spirit in the bond of peace" [130]

Another thing to understand is that when God does a new thing, not everyone automatically wants the new for many different reasons.

The new movement needs to humbly recognize this and not judge the establishment for not moving into the new. A judgmental attitude will be a snare and hinder the progress of the new.

Jesus says that if you have drunk old wine you do not immediately desire the new, because you like the old better!

A good example of this is that often-older people tend to prefer the older worship styles and songs. Wise is the pastor that has two services, one that accommodates the older people and one for the youngergeneration.

But the big question is how do we handle the new thing God is doing today? Jesus has the answer: *"new wine must be put into new wineskins".*

We need to accept that when God does a new thing, it must have a new structure! If not, both the new thing and the old structure will suffer loss.

That is very difficult for some leaders to accept. One reason is that they believe that church growth means more people in their buildings, instead of understanding

[130] Ephesus 4:3

that church growth is not addition but rather reproduction. In nature, we see that the fruit of an apple tree is not just more apples, but more apple trees!

God is concerned about the old church structure – the old wineskin as well as the new. In His mercy, He does not want the old structure to be destroyed but neither does He want the new structure/wineskin to be hindered!

I also believe God loves the main line churches and wants them to be fruitful by releasing their sons and daughters into the new structures.

God has not left the traditional local Church. No! But His heart is to renew and reactivated it.

He wants every local Church today to experience the dynamic, powerful, authentic Church life that we read about in the New Testament.

Our Lord is not coming for a handicapped Church that is wrapped in grave clothes. Jesus is coming for *"a glorious and holy church, without faults or spots or wrinkles or any other flaws".* (Ephesus 5:27 CEV)

Chapter Eighteen

Jesus Christ is still on the Earth today!

Many Christians do not realize that Jesus is still on this earth today. He is doing the same things today as He did in the Gospels. It is Luke, the author of Acts that reveals this hidden secret to us.

This is how Luke begins the book of Acts; *"In my first book, Theophilus, I wrote about what Jesus began to do and teach".*[131]

The word *"began"* carries a great message.
What Jesus began in the Gospels He carries on in the book of Acts, and the amazing thing is that the Son of Man has been living and working in His earthly spiritual Body now for more than 2000 years!

[131] Acts 1:1 GW

Throughout Church history, the One that has been behind all the ministry, works, and moves of God is Jesus Christ. It is He, living in His Body through the Holy Spirit, that has done all the works that we read about in Church history books.

Jesus sacrificed His earthly body on the cross but on the Day of Pentecost, the Father gave him a new body. That Body is *"the fullness of Him".*[132]

In the same way that the life of God filled Jesus' earthly body 2000 years ago, His life fills His spiritual Body today and He desires to express Himself through it.

Because we are His Body, we know that when someone touches us they also touch Him.

Paul experienced this on the road to Damascus when he encountered Jesus. Paul asked, *"who are you"?* The Lord answered, *"I am Jesus whom you persecute".*[133]

Did Paul then say "I am not persecuting you? I am persecuting the Christians"? No, Paul was given the revelation that if you touch a Christian, you have touched the Lord Himself.

The Head and the Body are one. It is not just the Christians' spirits that are one with the Lord, even their bodies are one with Him. The Bible says, *"your bodies are the members of Christ"*?[134] This is an awesome truth to ponder!

---

[132] Ephesians 1:23 MKJV
[133] Acts 9:5 MKJV
[134] 1Corinthens 6:15 MKJV

What Paul discovered was that every Christian is linked organically and homogeneously with Jesus Christ. This unity is incredible! Whatever Jesus is, we are! The Bible tells us, *"as he is, so are we in this world".* [135]

The awesome message that this fact carries is this: when an unbeliever encounters us, they also encounter Jesus Christ, the Son of God.

The Challenge

Our unity with the Lord is both a blessing and a challenge. With the blessing comes the awesome responsibility to allow the Lord to accomplish His will through us corporately.

However, in a way, one can say that Jesus has been locked inside His spiritual Body because of the Church's disobedience and unbelief. The Body has had parts that are paralyzed because they are unresponsive to the Head.

The Church has been like Lazarus in the Gospel of John.[136] Jesus spoke resurrection life into the tomb of Lazarus and the one that had been dead came out alive but bound. The grave clothes prevented Lazarus from moving freely. But Jesus commanded His disciples to *"Loose him, and let him go"*[137]

---

[135] 1John 4:17
[136] John 11:44
[137] John 11:44

That is a perfect picture of what has happened with the Church in the last 50-60 years. God has raised up different ministries that have heard the Lords command; "Loose my Body from its grave clothes and set her free!"

The Grave Clothes are coming off the Body of Christ

Let me give you an overview of recent decades leading to the healing of Christ's "handicapped" body.

During the 1960's God began to pour out His Spirit upon different mainline denominations. The outpouring was called the "Charismatic Movement."

Within the Catholic Church this movement made an enormous impact. In the United States alone there are an estimated 5.4 million Catholic charismatics. These Catholics have had a personal encounter with Jesus and believe strongly in the power of the Holy Spirit and His gifts.

During the 1970's thousands of prayer organizations in countless countries throughout the world were born out of this outpouring of the Holy Spirit.

Peter Wagner comments on this in his book, Spheres of Authority: "The decade of the 1970's saw the beginnings of the emergence of the enormous global prayer movement we see today. The body of Christ began to accept the gift and office of intercessor". [138]

---

[138] p.14

The Lord used these prayer movements to inspire millions of intercessors to pray for worldwide revival, and many intercessors at that time experienced the travailing prayer that Paul wrote about in Gal 4:19; *"My dear children! Once again, just like a mother in childbirth, I feel the same kind of pain for you until Christ's nature is formed in you".* [139]

During the 1980's the Lord gave birth through the world wide intercessors to the prophetic movement which has since then greatly impacted the church all over the world.

Bill Hamon summarizes this in his book, **The Day of the Saints**: "The movement was birthed in the United States of America and then spread around the world...The prophetic movement brought the revelation of how to activate saints into their spiritual gifts of prophecy, word of knowledge, and word of wisdom" [140]

During the 1990's we saw God begin to give birth to the apostolic movement. Prophets began to prophetically point out apostles and set them apart for their calling.

Today there are many apostolic networks in the United States which represent thousands of churches and ministries. Examples of these networks are: International Roundtable of Apostles (ICA), New Apostolic Roundtable (NAR), Eagles' Vision Apostolic-

---

[139] GNB
[140] p.163

Team. (AVAT). Global Spheres, Inc. (GSI) in Corinth, Texas.

What we see today also is that God is uniting all of these movements to usher in the establishment of the Kingdom of God on the earth!

Let me give the statistics that prove that the grave clothes have come off the Body of Christ. Researchers estimate that: [141]

- Every 25 min. 3000 people are coming to Christ. That means that around the globe every day 175,000 people are coming to Christ. What happened on the day of Pentecost was just a foretaste.

- There are currently 60-80 million Christians in China with between10,000-25,000 converts a day.

- In the one area of China's Henan province, over 90% of the people are Christians.

- Between 1990 and 2004, the number of Christians in Cambodia grew from 200 to 400,000

- 44% of the people of Guatemala are "born-again Christians". In neighboring El Salvador the number is at 53.6%.

[141] Source for the statistics: Open Door, Vision 2020, William Stearns, Operation World, Campus Crusade and Wycliffe.

- More Muslims have turned to Christ in the last ten years than in the previous 1,000 years.

- On June 15th, 2006, 3,000,000 believers paraded through Sao Paolo, Brazil in the world's largest "March for Jesus".

- The number of Christians in Indonesia has grown from 1.3M forty years ago to over 11M today.

- By 2042 every people group on this earth will have the Bible translated into their language.

- The Jesus Film has been translated into nearly 1000 languages and over 200,000,000 people have indicated decisions for Christ as a result of the film.

- No Christian was officially allowed to live in Nepal until 1960. Now there is a church in every one of the 75 districts of Nepal with estimates of over half a million believers.

- In A.D. 100, there were 360 non-Christians for every true believer. Today the ratio is less than seven to every believer.

- Every day, 20,000 Africans come to Christ. Africa was 3% Christian in 1900 and is now over 50% Christian.

- In 1900 Korea had no Protestant church and the country was deemed impossible to penetrate. Today Korea is 30% Christian with 7000 churches in Seoul alone and several of these churches have over 1,000,000 members.

- The government of Papua, New Guinea mandated Bible teaching in every school in the country.

These Statistics are a Great Sign that Jesus is Coming Soon for His Church.

Our Lord is not coming for a handicapped Church that is wrapped in grave clothes. Jesus is coming for *"a glorious and holy church, without faults or spots or wrinkles or any other flaws".*[142]

Over the years we have heard many prophecies about the exceedingly great harvest of souls that the Church will reap in the last days before the second coming of Jesus.

Now is the time to see fulfillment of those prophetic words.

Now is also the time for the Church to do greater works when what Jesus did. [143]

Today the nations are beginning to see and know that Jesus, the most powerful person in history, has come out from the grave, and that the grave clothes have been taken off the Body of Christ.

---

142 Ephesus 5:27 CEV

143 Joh 14:12

Because of this fact, in the next few years we will see the greatest move of God ever. Millions and millions of people will turn to God.

"You say, don't you, 'In four more months the harvest will begin?' Look, I tell you, open your eyes and observe that the fields are ready for harvesting now"! [144]

Today God's glory is rising over His people

The prophetic word for our time is this; *"Arise, shine; for your light has come, and the glory of Jehovah has risen on you. For behold, the darkness shall cover the earth, and gross darkness the peoples; but Jehovah shall rise on you, and His glory shall be seen on you"*[145]

This word is telling us two things:

1. *"Darkness shall cover the earth, and gross darkness the peoples".*

2. *"Jehovah shall rise on you, and His glory shall be seen on you".*

In other words, God is dealing with the nations in one way and with the people of God in a completely different way.

[144] Joh 4:35 ISV

[145] Isa 60:1-2 MKJV

Gods dealing with the Nations

As I write this (June 10, 2016) we have had 10 major floods in the United States since last September. Never before in U.S. history have we been hit with so many floods in such a short time.

The last few years, the weather has gone crazy not just in our nation but also in many other nations.

Romans 8:22 and 19 tells us that the *"whole creation groans and labors with birth pangs"* and that it *"eagerly awaits the revelation of the sons of God."*

It is not just the weather that the nations have to contend with. This year Venezuela has had a 700 % devaluation of their currencies. The effect has been riots in the streets and many families going without the necessary food for themselves and for their children because the shelves in the stores are empty.

Furthermore, both Greece and Puerto Rico have gone bankrupt and from the current economic statistics, other countries are sure to follow.

Nevertheless, we know that God can use these difficult times to prepare and open the nations to receive the visitation that He is getting ready to send to the people that humble themselves and cry out to Him.

Now is time for "the latter rain" and for "the best wine".

We are living today in a world that is beginning to shake like never before. The global events are more or less out of control.

The word of God tells us; "*When God spoke to your ancestors, his voice shook the earth. But now he has promised, "Once more I will shake not only the earth but also the sky." The words once more show clearly that God will change what he has made. These are the things that can be shaken. Then only the things that cannot be shaken will remain".*[146]

Millions of people are going to search for answers. The number one topic that they are going to be interestedin is: what does the Bible tell us about the end times? They are going to want to know why this earth has gone nuts!

The lukewarm Church with the "me-centered" gospel will not give them the answer.

The answer for the people of the nations and their governments will be the reborn and restored dynamic Church of the New Testament!

The Church in the end times will begin its mission of *"disciple all the nations".*[147]

For many years, the war cry of the Church has been: "Jesus is the answer". I want to change that war cry to: "The Christ is the answer".

---

[146] Heb 12:26-27 GW

[147] Mat 28:19 YLT

Christ is not just the Head; Christ is the Head and the Body working together in unprecedented unity and harmony and glorious power! [148]

Christ is the one new man which is Messianic Jews and born again Gentiles together, the new man that the Lord created by His cross. [149]

"The Christ" is the answer for all the shakings that are coming upon this earth. The destiny of this earth lies in the hands of "The Christ" of whom Paul speaks; *"Having made known unto us the mystery of his will...That in the dispensation of the fullness of times he might gather together in one all things in Christ".* [150]

[148] 1Corinthen 12:12

[149] Ephesus 2:15

[150] Ephesus; 1:9-10

Amen, Lord Jesus!
Let the love revolution begin!

Chapter Nineteen

A Love Revolution

Ingmar Kjellstrom, who is now with the Lord, was a Swedish brother in Christ that I met at the end of the 60's. Ingmar was a single man who became very attached to me and to my first wife, Elsa (who is in heaven), and our five children. He became such a part of our family that when we moved to another town, he moved with us. He remained a part of our family for about 30 years and was like a grandfather to the children. He truly was an example of a single man of God who found his purpose through family.

Ingmar was one of the most loyal friends I have ever had. He was also an incredibly faithful personal intercessor for me. Only in heaven will I know all that God protected me from and provided for me because of this wonderful brother's intercession. I sense he is still praying!

When Ingmar came into his late 70's, we began to notice that dementia was setting in. He began to ask the same questions repeatedly and began to lose the amazingly sharp mind he had once had. He had learned to speak several languages in his life.

But one message that the Lord had burned deeply in his heart for years, never waned nor became dull. That was the passage of John 17 in which Jesus prayed to His Father that we, God's people, would be one as He and the Father are one.

Even as his dementia became Alzheimer's, he could still quote the passage from memory and he would always end by saying, "The Lord is getting ready to ignite a love revolution!"

My brother Ingmar went home to Jesus on September 17, 1993 on what would have been Elsa's 50th birthday. I'm sure she welcomed him home!

Nevertheless, though Ingmar has been gone now for 23 years, I can still hear his message echoing loud and clear all the way to today; "the Lord is getting ready to ignite a love revolution!"

Amen,
Lord Jesus!

LET THE LOVE
REVOLUTION

BEGIN!

Thanks

I want to thank my wife Berta without whose help this book could not have come to fruition. She turned my "Swinglish" into correct English and also put her own touch on the book. She has been more than my editor.

I also what to thank Karin Lynn-Hill for her technical work. And all the work she has done for me and Berta.

ABOUT THE AUTHOR

Rune Brännström is a native of Sweden who for the past 17 years has resided with his wife, Berta, in her hometown of San Antonio, Texas.

Rune is a pastor and leads a weekly pastor fellowship. In addition, he is the founder and the director of Nehemiah Initiative, a prayer evangelization movement for revival and transformation.(Nehemiahinitiative.com)

In the 1970's Rune founded an Eastern European Mission and took initiative to youth and Jesus Festivals in Sweden, which gathered 10,000 – 15,000 people. He also co-founded a national monthly Christian publication and a Bible school in Sweden.

In the 1980's he arranged conferences in East Europe together with local leaders, which gathered thousands of Catholics and Protestants in unity to exalt Jesus.

In the 1990's, Rune organized evangelistic outreaches, with others in Macedonia and Serbia. This led to the planting of a church in Skopje, Macedonia which is still thriving today. The leaders of that Church are planting other churches.

In September of 1999 he moved from Sweden to San Antonio with his wife Berta to serve the Lord there and to join others in working towards city transformation. In the year 2000 they planted a church in the inner city among Hispanics which today is called The King's Mission Fellowship.

For more information, write to:

Rune Brannstrom
12531 Course View,
San Antonio, Texas 78221, USA
E-mailrunebrannstrom@hotmail.com

Also by Rune Brännström

The Secrets of King David Unveiled
(New Life Celebration Publisher)

To read a free sample chapter, go to:
http://www.bookdaily.com/book/4702512

THIS BOOK REVEALS SECRETS

- How to unlock heaven by the key of David
- Discover why Seventy-Seven Chapters in the Bible are about King David and his kingdom

- Find the secret behind the greatest manifestation of the Kingdom of God in the Old Testament
- Uncover how David establish the throne of God on the earth
- Understand how to realize the Holy Spirit's Power through the Ark of God
- Learn how to transform our cities and nation

This Book can give you a new paradigm shift. For several decades many cities have had Citywide Christian events with the goal of city transformation. No effort in any city has fully succeeded. Why? Could it be that we have not followed the example God has given us in the Bible?

The Artist

A very gifted 20-year-old girl has done the art work for the cover of this book. Her name is Kristian Lynn Villareal and her family has recently become members of our Church.

I was not aware of how gifted an artist Kristian was. She told me that she was an art student and when I heard that, without seeing any of her paintings, I felt led to ask her to do the cover of my book. I gave her some ideas, but what she has created is beyond my expectations. It is a prophetic painting.

This is the message that this painting carries:

1. The lion is ready to roar through His Church! "*Jehovah will roar from Zion* [The Church] *and utter His voice from Jerusalem*"[151]

[151] Amos 1:2 MKJV

2. When the Lamp stand - the Church[152] - is set ablaze with the fire of God's love, Israel the Jewish state - the star of David - will be ignited by that fire.

3. Although a lion is by nature a fierce animal, this Lion's eyes are filled with love. It is proclaiming that the Lion of Judah is rising up within in His Church with the power of His love. Through the Church, ablaze with His love, He is getting ready to come against the Enemy with a mighty Roar!

This painting was a gift from Kristian and today it hangs in our church on the wall in the foyer. It is the first thing you see as you enter the church.

To contact Kristian Lynn Villareal

Email: klynn.arts@gmail.com

[152] The Lampstand in Revelation 1:20 is the Church

PERMISSIONS

WNT *-* ***Weymouth New Testament*** *in Modern Speech Second Edition 1912 Public Domain--Copy Freely*

Scriptures marked ***BBE*** *are taken from the* ***1965 Bible in Basic English –*** *Public Domain – Copy Freely*

Scriptures marked ***ESV*** *are taken from the THE HOLY BIBLE,* ***ENGLISH STANDARD VERSION*** *(ESV): Scriptures taken from THE HOLY BIBLE, ENGLISH STANDARD VERSION ® Copyright© 2001 by Crossway, a publishing ministry of Good News Publishers. Used by permission.*

Scriptures marked ***LITV*** *are taken from the* ***Literal Translation of the Holy Bible*** *Copyright© 1976 - 2000 By Jay P. Green, Sr. Used by permission of the copyright holder Courtesy of Sovereign Grace Publishers and Christian Literature World*

Scriptures marked ***NIV*** *are taken from the* ***NEW INTERNATIONAL VERSION*** *(NIV): Scripture taken from THE HOLY BIBLE, NEW INTERNATIONAL VERSION ®. Copyright© 1973, 1978, 1984, 2011 by Biblica, Inc.™. Used by permission of Zondervan*

Scriptures quotations marked ***JUB*** *are taken from the* ***Jubilee Bible*** *(or Biblia del Jubileo), copyright © 2000, 2001, 2010, 2013 by Life Sentence Publishing, Inc. Used by permission of Life Sentence Publishing, Inc., Abbotsford, Wisconsin. All rights reserved.*

Scriptures marked ***YLT*** *are from 1898* ***Young's Literal Translation Bible*** *(Public Domain)*

Made in the USA
San Bernardino, CA
12 January 2017